JAMES E. TALMAGE'S

JESUS
THE
CHRIST
STUDY GUIDE

JAMES E. TALMAGE
1862–1933

JAMES E. TALMAGE'S

JESUS
THE
CHRIST
STUDY GUIDE

RICHARD NEITZEL HOLZAPFEL

THOMAS A. WAYMENT

DESERET
BOOK

Salt Lake City, Utah

Library of Congress Cataloging-in-Publication Data

Holzapfel, Richard Neitzel, 1954– author.
   Jesus the Christ study guide / Richard Neitzel Holzapfel and Thomas A. Wayment.
     pages cm
   Includes bibliographical references.
   ISBN 978-1-60907-937-6 (paperbound)
1. Talmage, James E. (James Edward), 1862–1933. Jesus the Christ. 2. The Church of Jesus Christ of Latter-day Saints—Doctrines. 3. Mormon Church—Doctrines. 4. Jesus Christ—Biography. I. Wayment, Thomas A., author. II. Title.
   BX8643.J4T334 2014
   232.088'2893—dc23   2014015289

Printed in the United States of America
Publishers Printing, Salt Lake City, UT

10 9 8 7 6 5 4 3 2 1

CONTENTS

PART 3: THE PUBLIC MINISTRY BEGINS

PART 4: THE SERMON ON THE MOUNT
AND THE MISSION OF THE TWELVE

PART 5: REJECTION OF JESUS IN GALILEE AND JERUSALEM

PART 6: FINAL DAYS IN JERUSALEM

PART 7: LAST SUPPER TO THE RESURRECTION

PART 8: THE APOSTASY TO THE SECOND COMING

PREFACE

This study guide is meant to supplement, not to replace or duplicate, the material in Elder James E. Talmage's *Jesus the Christ*. We envision you with a copy of *Jesus the Christ* in one hand, this study guide in the other, and the scriptures in front of you. Using this guide, we hope you will carefully read *Jesus the Christ* and look up the scripture references, so you can take full advantage of Elder Talmage's most important book.

When a study guide was prepared in 1916 for use in the Melchizedek Priesthood and priests quorums, the writing committee identified three goals for readers of *Jesus the Christ:*

1. Enlarge our knowledge of facts.

2. Increase our faith in the divine mission of the Son of God.

3. Learn the doctrines of the plan of salvation.

Another study guide to *Jesus the Christ,* published serially in the *Instructor* magazine, was prepared for use in the Church's

1964 Sunday School program. In that guide, the following goals were explained:

"Our study this year is going to take us beyond the study of a single book. Elder Talmage based his writing mainly on the scriptures, particularly on the Gospels in the New Testament which portray the life of Jesus Christ briefly, but with artistry and conviction. We, too, shall be led back to the original sources. However, our main purpose will be neither a study of Brother Talmage's work nor of the Gospels. These are but means to an end, the vehicles by which we see our goal. Our study this year is of Jesus Christ, Himself—His life, His teachings, and His mission among men. We would come to know Him more fully for He is the head of our Church, the chief cornerstone of our faith. We belong to His church, bear witness to His Gospel, and aspire to be His disciples. Even the study of Jesus Christ, Himself, is not our ultimate goal this year. We wish to go beyond study and come into a new relationship with our Lord and Saviour. We seek His companionship, the sweet influence of His Holy Spirit. We would that under this influence, our lives might change, that we might find new goals, establish finer relations with loved ones, associates, and mankind; and that the quality of our faith, repentance, humility, and love might improve" (1963–64 Study Guide, 406).

We invite you to consider these timeless goals as you begin your study of *Jesus the Christ.*

ACKNOWLEDGMENTS

We express our sincere thanks and appreciation to all those who assisted us along the way.

We extend our special thanks to those who read the manuscript—Matthew Grey, Robert L. Millet, and D. Kelly Ogden. Ted Stoddard, one of our most helpful colleagues, read the manuscript several times, helping us refine our thinking and assisting us to produce the glossary found at the end of this volume.

Additionally, several other colleagues, including Lincoln H. Blumell, S. Kent Brown, Kent P. Jackson, Frank Judd, Gaye Strathearn, and John W. Welch, provided ideas for us to consider as we prepared this study guide and have, through our association, encouraged us to think in new ways. Their suggestions regarding style, organization, and content have significantly improved this work. As always, we appreciate the encouragement we have received from our colleagues in many untold ways. We are especially appreciative of the support we received from Religious Education at Brigham Young University.

We thank our Brigham Young University student assistants, Devin Butler, Jessica Coleman, Hannah Murray, Ben Nielsen, Leah Smartt, Sarah Thompson, and Joseph Wright, for their contributions in researching and source checking. We also asked them to read *Jesus the Christ* and mark their questions in the text—a procedure that was invaluable in helping us know where we might assist other readers to more fully appreciate Elder Talmage's work.

We are grateful to Deseret Book for the invitation to pursue this project, and we appreciate working with them, especially Lisa Roper, Suzanne Brady, Shauna Gibby, and Malina Grigg.

Above all others, we thank our wives, Jeni Holzapfel and Brandi Wayment, who have patiently endured long days and nights, incessant interruptions, and early-morning and late-night telephone calls. We cannot adequately express our appreciation to them for their support through "just one more revision" and then listening to our pleas for their continued support for future projects. Without their encouragement and sacrifice, our work would not be possible. Our children also have been patient and understanding as we ran another research and writing marathon.

INTRODUCTION TO
JESUS THE CHRIST AND
THIS STUDY GUIDE

Jesus the Christ is truly a Latter-day Saint classic. It is found on bookshelves in the homes of many members of The Church of Jesus Christ of Latter-day Saints and carried throughout the world by tens of thousands of missionaries every year. In September 2015, we celebrate the one hundredth anniversary of its publication.

With well over a million copies printed since 1915, *Jesus the Christ* was written at the request of the First Presidency and published by the Church. In 1962, President Marion G. Romney, then of the Quorum of the Twelve Apostles, observed, "[*Jesus the Christ*] enjoys an authoritative endorsement such as few books enjoy" ("Book," 866).

Additionally, *Jesus the Christ* is the only book that has been written in the Salt Lake Temple, making it a truly distinctive work.

The full title is *Jesus the Christ: A Study of the Messiah and His*

Mission according to Holy Scriptures Both Ancient and Modern. It was written "By James E. Talmage: One of the Twelve Apostles of The Church of Jesus Christ of Latter-day Saints."

Throughout this guide, page numbers in parentheses refer to pages of the edition of *Jesus the Christ* published officially by the Church. Because other editions have different pagination, the page numbers in the copy you use may not correspond exactly; however, the chapter designations are the same in all editions, so you will be able to find the content referred to in this study guide by checking the specific chapter.

PRAISE AND RECOMMENDATIONS FOR *JESUS THE CHRIST*

In August 1915, just before *Jesus the Christ* was published, the First Presidency—Joseph F. Smith, Anthon H. Lund, and Charles W. Penrose—announced the following:

"The sacred subject of our Savior's life and mission is presented as it is accepted and proclaimed by the Church that bears His Holy Name. We desire that the work, 'Jesus the Christ,' be read and studied by the Latter-day Saints, in their families, and in the organizations that are devoted wholly or in part to theological study. We commend it especially for use in our Church schools, as also for the advanced theological classes in Sunday schools and priesthood quorums, for the instruction of our missionaries, and for general reading" ("Official Announcement," *Deseret Evening News,* 14 August 1915, 4).

At the time of Elder Talmage's death in 1933, Elder Melvin J. Ballard of the Quorum of the Twelve Apostles reflected upon Elder Talmage's legacy: "He produced many volumes that shall be read until the end of time, because that which he has written is so clear and so impressive that it shall ever be among the cherished treasures for those who love the works of God. Yet these contributions he gave freely to the Church without any earthly reward" ("Full Report of Talmage Funeral Given," *Deseret News,* 5 August 1933, 1).

President Marion G. Romney, then of the Quorum of the Twelve Apostles, noted in 1962: "One who gets the understanding, the vision, and the spirit of the resurrected Lord through a careful study of the text *Jesus the Christ* by Elder James E. Talmage will find that he has greatly increased his moving faith in our glorified Redeemer" ("Book," 868).

GENERAL CONFERENCES

Prophets and Apostles have continued to quote and refer to *Jesus the Christ* in general conference addresses, another indication of its continuing influence. See, for example, President Spencer W. Kimball, President of the Church (April 1978); Elder Neal A. Maxwell of the Quorum of the Twelve Apostles (April 1989); President Howard W. Hunter, President of the Quorum of the Twelve Apostles (October 1990); Elder David B. Haight of the Quorum of the Twelve Apostles (April 1994); Elder Russell M. Nelson of the Quorum of the Twelve Apostles (April 1995); Elder Robert D. Hales of the Quorum of the Twelve Apostles (April 2003); Elder Quentin L. Cook of the Quorum of the Twelve Apostles (April 2010); President Thomas S. Monson, President of the Church (April 2010); and Elder D. Todd Christofferson of the Quorum of the Twelve Apostles (April 2014). Additionally, members of the Seventy and general Church officers often quote Elder Talmage in general conference addresses; a recent example is Sister Linda S. Reeves of the Relief Society General Presidency (October 2012).

CONTRIBUTIONS

Elder James E. Talmage was the first Latter-day Saint to write a full-length study of the Savior's life and ministry, and in it he provides a Restoration perspective. This approach separated him from all other contemporary books on the life of Christ. Elder Talmage noted, "It will be readily seen that the author has departed from the course usually followed by writers on the Life of Jesus Christ, which course as a rule, begins with the birth of Mary's Babe and ends with the ascension of the slain and risen Lord from Olivet" (iii).

The most enduring legacy of *Jesus the Christ* may well be its record of Elder Talmage's personal testimony and witness of the divine Sonship of Jesus Christ.

ACCEPTANCE AND POPULARITY

The immediate acceptance and popularity of *Jesus the Christ* following its publication in September 1915 are demonstrated by the release of a second edition just three months later, in December 1915. A third edition, with new notes and references, demonstrating Elder Talmage's efforts to update his work, appeared in March 1916; this edition was followed almost immediately with fourth and fifth editions before the end of that year.

More editions followed. In 1922, Elder Talmage recorded in his journal the release of yet another edition of *Jesus the Christ:* "Today I received a copy of the book 'Jesus the Christ,' sixth edition, including the 30th thousand. This edition has been printed at the Deseret News establishment from the electroplates used in earlier issues, with some corrections of typographical errors and other minor changes. Both in printing and in binding the new book presents a very attractive appearance. The work has been 'out of print' for months past" (23 November 1922, L. Tom

Perry Special Collections, Harold B. Lee Library, Brigham Young University, Provo, Utah).

By 1965, on the fiftieth anniversary of its publication, the thirty-fourth edition of *Jesus the Christ* was in print.

Eventually translated into more than fifteen languages, *Jesus the Christ* is also available in English braille, as an audiobook on CDs, as an eBook, and as an MP3 file. Numerous editions are currently available, including illustrated, leather-bound, paperback, hardcover, compact, and special collectors' editions. *Jesus the Christ* is published by several companies in addition to The Church of Jesus Christ of Latter-day Saints. It is available for download from the Church's official webpage, jesuschrist.lds.org (http://www.lds .org/media-library/audio-interim/jesus-the-christ?lang=eng).

JAMES EDWARD TALMAGE, 1862–1933

A third-generation Latter-day Saint, James Edward Talmage was born in Hungerford, Berkshire, England, on 21 September 1862. The Talmage family eventually left England and moved to Utah, where they arrived on 19 June 1876. They settled in Provo, Utah County, Utah. There, young James attended the recently established Brigham Young Academy (BYA), now known as Brigham Young University.

James completed course work necessary to receive a normal (teaching) diploma from BYA in 1881. To gain further education than was then available in Utah, he attended Lehigh University in Pennsylvania during the 1882–83 academic year, studying chemistry and geology; the next year he attended Johns Hopkins University in Maryland, where he completed advanced classes. He returned to Utah in 1884 and began teaching at BYA, participating in local politics, and fulfilling a variety of Church assignments.

In June 1888, James married Merry May Booth in the Manti Temple. Eight children, four sons and four daughters, were eventually born to the couple.

The same year as his marriage, James was appointed as principal of the Salt Lake Stake Academy, later known as the Latter-day Saints' College and known today as LDS Business College. He served as principal until 1894, when he was appointed president of the University of Deseret (now University of Utah). During his service as president, he earned a PhD from Wesleyan University in Illinois as a nonresident in 1896. In 1897, he left his position as president of the University of Utah to become a geological and mining consultant, but he continued as a professor of geology at the University of Utah until 1907.

By 1900, James E. Talmage had become a well-known and respected scientist, educator, author, and school administrator. Among the honors he received were membership as a Fellow of the Royal Society of Edinburgh, Fellow of the Royal Microscopic Society, Fellow of the Royal Geological Society, Associate of the Philosophical Society of Great Britain, or Victoria Institute, and Fellow of the American Association for the Advancement of Science.

Brother Talmage's Church work continued uninterrupted. While he was principal of the Latter-day Saints' College, the First Presidency asked him to deliver a series of lectures on the doctrines of the Church. These lectures were published in the Church's *Juvenile Instructor* magazine. Eventually gathered into a book, they were published in 1899 as *The Articles of Faith*. This book became one of the most important, definitive works on Latter-day Saint doctrine and practice at that time.

His Church assignments included preparing, under the direction of the First Presidency, a new edition of the Pearl of Great

Price, published in 1902. Two years later, the First Presidency asked him to deliver lectures on the life of Jesus Christ and to publish those lectures. He continued to write books about Church doctrines, beliefs, and practices. *The Great Apostasy* was published in 1909, before his call to the Quorum of the Twelve Apostles. Between his call to the apostleship and the publication of *Jesus the Christ*, Elder Talmage published *The House of the Lord,* 1912; *The Story and Philosophy of Mormonism,* 1914; and *The Philosophical Basis of Mormonism,* 1915.

James E. Talmage was called to the Quorum of the Twelve Apostles in December 1911; he served diligently until his death in July 1933. During his apostolic ministry, Elder Talmage helped prepare a scripture index for missionaries, called "Ready References," in 1916, a new edition of the Book of Mormon in 1920, and new editions of the Doctrine and Covenants and Pearl of Great Price in 1921. He presided over the Church's European Mission from 1924 to 1928.

After his death in 1933, Elder Talmage's influence continued, primarily through three of his books: *The Articles of Faith, House of the Lord,* and *Jesus the Christ.* The effect and reach of these books cannot be overestimated. For many Latter-day Saints, *Jesus the Christ* is the first book-length study on the life of Christ they read.

PUBLICATION OF *JESUS THE CHRIST*

In September 1904, Brother Talmage noted in his journal a decision that led to a later request from the First Presidency: "Forenoon committee meeting and afternoon consultation regarding University Sunday School. Decided to conduct the work this year as lecture courses, of which there will be one on the

Book of Mormon by Brother John M. Mills, and one on the subject 'Jesus The Christ' by myself" (18 September 1904).

On Sundays in Salt Lake City between 1904 and 1906,
Brother Talmage delivered forty-two lectures on the life and ministry of Jesus Christ. In preparation for those lectures, Brother
Talmage read and studied a number of Protestant New Testament
scholarly works in English, a practice he had started much earlier during his writing career by applying his academic skills to
his interest in biblical studies. He read extensively from sources
that enabled him to become familiar with New Testament scholarship and issues and debates associated with the rise of modern
biblical studies. He was a serious and competent scientist, which
allowed him to analyze thoughtfully and synthesize a remarkably
vast amount of information as he prepared his lectures.

Among the works he studied were Frederic W. Farrar's *The
Life of Christ* (1874), Cunningham Geikie's two-volume *The Life
and Words of Christ* (1877), Alfred Edersheim's two-volume *The
Life and Times of Jesus the Messiah* (1883), Charles F. Deems's *The
Light of the Nations* (1884), and Samuel J. Andrews's *The Life of
Our Lord upon the Earth* (rev. ed., 1891). He also carefully re-
viewed several Bible dictionaries, including William Smith's
Dictionary of the Bible (1863).

Farrar, Geikie, and Edersheim, in particular, influenced
Brother Talmage's reconstruction of the first century, including
the cultural, religious, and social setting of Jesus Christ's ministry.
All were Anglican clergymen, teachers, and scholars, Edersheim
having converted from Judaism to Christianity earlier in his life.
They were familiar with ancient languages and had been formally
educated in biblical and related studies. In that sense, they were
experts, writing and teaching in fields they had been trained to

work in during their academic careers, and they also expressed in their writings a strong faith in the divinity of Jesus Christ.

Through the Protestant works he studied, Brother Talmage was introduced to some important ancient sources, including the intertestamental books of the Maccabees from the Apocrypha; the writings of the first-century Jewish historian Josephus; the writings of the first- and second-century Roman historians Suetonius and Tacitus; the Mishnah, an important Jewish text dating from the third century; the equally important Talmud, dating from the fourth and fifth centuries; and the fourth-century Christian writings of Eusebius.

At that time, a small but important group of scholars had begun questioning the reliability of the New Testament and its account of Jesus's miracles, including the Resurrection. In response, Brother Talmage prepared a Latter-day Saint interpretation of the life and ministry of Jesus the Christ, an undertaking that testified of the truths of the New Testament and specifically of the mission of God's Son.

As the lecture series on the Savior continued, the First Presidency—Joseph F. Smith, John R. Winder, and Anthon H. Lund—asked Brother Talmage, who had not yet been called to the Quorum of the Twelve Apostles, to turn his popular addresses into a book. Brother Talmage noted in his diary in August 1905: "In the course of the interview with the First Presidency, I was handed the attached letter, which has been awaiting me since the date thereof. Compliance with the request will require much time as not half the lectures have been delivered and not a line of one of them written, except as class notes" (9 August 1905). The letter stated, "We should be pleased to have you print and publish in book form the course of lectures being delivered by you before the University Sunday School on the subject, Jesus the Christ, believing they will prove a valuable acquisition to our Church Literature, and that the proposed work should be placed within the reach of Church members and general readers" (Joseph F. Smith et al. to James E. Talmage, 18 July 1905).

For a variety of reasons, including a request by the First Presidency to write *House of the Lord: A Study of Ancient and Modern Temples* (1912), Elder Talmage was unable to begin the assignment to write *Jesus the Christ* in earnest until 1914, three years after he was called to the Quorum of the Twelve Apostles. That year he noted the following in his journal:

> During the school periods of 1904–1905, and 1905–1906, I delivered a series of lectures entitled "Jesus the Christ," under the auspices of the University Sunday School. The sessions were held during Sunday forenoons in Barratt Hall. I received written appointment from the First Presidency to embody the lectures in a book to be published for the use of the Church in general. Work on this appointment has been suspended from time to time owing to other duties being imposed upon me. Lately, however, I have been asked to prepare the matter for the book with as little delay as possible. Experiences demonstrated that neither in my comfortable office nor in the convenient study room at home can I be free from visits and telephone calls, in consequence of this condition, and in view of the importance of the work, I have been directed to occupy a room in the Temple where I will be free from interruption. I began the work in the Temple today and hope that I shall be able to devote the necessary time thereto. (14 September 1914.)

As he prepared the manuscript, Elder Talmage borrowed and adapted material from the Protestant writers and scholars he had carefully read and studied for more than a decade. Although he was not a trained biblical scholar, had not studied ancient biblical languages, and had not visited the sites associated with Jesus Christ's life and ministry, he was interested in the knowledge scholars could provide as background to the story of Jesus Christ. He was most interested, however, in providing what they could not—an apostolic testimony of the divine mission of Jesus Christ. And because of his Church experience, his calling as an Apostle, and his assignment from the First Presidency of the Church to write *The Articles of Faith,* he had a thorough command of Church doctrine.

In addition to both the Old and the New Testaments, Elder Talmage quoted from the scriptures of the Restoration, including the Book of Mormon, the Doctrine and Covenants, and the Pearl of Great Price. He noted this significant aspect of his work, something that separated his book from other studies about the life of Jesus Christ, saying, "A characteristic feature of the work is the guidance afforded by modern scripture and the explication of the Holy Writ of olden times in the light of present day revelation, which, as a powerful and well directed beam, illumines many dark passages of ancient construction" (iv).

Elder Talmage also drew from his own published works, including *The Articles of Faith* (1899), *The Great Apostasy* (1909), *House of the Lord* (1912), and *The Story and Philosophy of Mormonism* (1914).

Many of his earlier addresses, articles, and books had drawn on the same biblical scholars Elder Talmage relied upon in writing *Jesus the Christ.* He was thus acquainted with conservative Protestant scholarship and some of the issues debated by New

Testament scholars at the time (see, for example, 422). He approached biblical studies as a moderate, avoiding the extreme positions caused by the polarizing effects of biblical scholarship in the United States at the time. It is important to note that his use of the term "critic," when referring to biblical scholars, is not negative (see, for example, 668). Elder Talmage uses the word as it was understood in academic circles: a biblical critic is someone who studies, analyzes, and interprets biblical texts and related fields, such as archaeology and papyrology.

He was not opposed to scholarly approaches to the study of the Bible and tried to find a balance between human reason and faith in the divine. For example, Elder Talmage knew that textual advances and discoveries made in the four centuries since the publication of the King James Version (KJV) allowed scholars to get much closer to the original readings of the text of the New Testament. Because no original manuscripts survived, only copies of copies of copies were available to the King James translators. Important manuscript discoveries made after 1611, when the KJV was first published, allow a closer approximation of the original biblical text better than ever before.

Recognizing such advances in New Testament manuscript studies, Elder Talmage quoted the 1881 Revised Version, which included recent discoveries and alternative readings, more than twenty times when he felt the readings were superior to the King James Version, which is identified as the common text or authorized version in *Jesus the Christ* (see, for example, 147, 228, 311, 366, 384, 446, 465, 481, 483, 488–89, 500–501, 512, 557, 596–97, 658, 696, 701–2, and 719). He candidly observed that in some cases he faced the impossibility of resolving textual problems. For example, he writes regarding the hour of the Crucifixion: "All attempts to harmonize the accounts [between the synoptic Gospels and the Gospel of John] in this particular have proved futile because the discrepancies are real" (668).

Throughout *Jesus the Christ,* readers may see Elder Talmage's efforts to take advantage of scholarship to provide context for his story. In a number of cases, he presents two sides of an issue (not an issue that affects the general story line or the major issues regarding Jesus's mission) and then tells his readers that he cannot, based on the sources at hand, reach a definitive conclusion on that particular issue (see, for example, 521).

Of course, Elder Talmage's interest is much larger than a scholarly debate about the text or the social, cultural, and religious setting of Jesus's ministry. He begins his study of *Jesus the Christ* by saying, "It is a matter of history that, at or near the beginning of what has since come to be known as the Christian era, the Man Jesus surnamed the Christ, was born in Bethlehem of Judea" (1). He adds, "As to who and what He was there are dissensions of grave moment dividing the opinions of men" (1).

In *Jesus the Christ,* Elder Talmage answers questions about the meaning of Christ's life and ministry while he also discusses the historical certainties generally accepted about that life. He begins his study from a position of faith in Jesus Christ as the divine Son of God, Savior, and Redeemer. His own testimony and witness provide the lens through which he reads and interprets the sources available to study the life of Jesus Christ.

Elder Talmage was well known for his disciplined work habits, so it is not surprising that he completed the manuscript in a little more than seven months, between 14 September 1914 and 19 April 1915. His son John R. Talmage remembered: "[I overheard] a friend of Father's expressing amazement that the writing had been concluded in so short a time, and Father replying to the effect that the period of preparation of the book had extended over more than a decade, during which time he had conducted extensive studies and research and developed his own thoughts and approaches. The seven-month period was merely devoted to setting down on paper the ideas that had developed and matured over the longer interval" ("Assignment," 807).

Elder Talmage noted in his journal: "[I] devoted every possible hour to the labor, oft-times working in the Temple until a late hour at night" (30 September 1914). His journals reveal that he worked on holidays: "Had Thanksgiving dinner with the family and spent the rest of the day until a late hour in the evening at the office" (26 November 1914); "Christmas Day. After taking part in the morning rejoicing and enjoying the pleasure of the children at their Christmas Tree and its fruit, I went to the office and spent a few hours in writing" (25 December 1914); and "Lincoln's Birthday. I devoted the day to writing on the book" (12 February 1915).

Elder Talmage spent time studying on Sundays but apparently did not write on Sundays: "Wife and I attended Fast meeting in the Temple and during the forenoon; and I remained in the Temple engaged in scriptural study during the rest of the day" (7 February 1915).

In April 1915, Elder Talmage noted: "Finished the actual writing on the book, 'Jesus The Christ,' to which I have devoted every spare hour since settling down to the work of composition on September 14th last. Had it not been that I was privileged to do this work in the Temple it would be at present far from completion. I have felt the inspiration of the place and have appreciated the privacy and quietness incident thereto. I hope to proceed with the work of revision without delay" (19 April 1915). His son observed, "The manuscript was penciled in longhand and is still in existence" (*Talmage Story,* 182).

Elder Talmage spent the next two months reading the finished manuscript to the First Presidency, members of the Quorum of the Twelve Apostles, and other Church leaders. In June 1915, he recorded: "At an early meeting of the First Presidency and Twelve. I read the last installment of the matter for the book. This was the eighteenth sitting of the council to hear the reading of the manuscript" (24 June 1915).

Finally, Elder Talmage announced in September 1915, "Today I had the pleasure of presenting to the First Presidency the first three copies of the book 'Jesus The Christ' to leave the bindery" (9 September 1915).

AFTER ONE HUNDRED YEARS

One hundred years have passed since Elder Talmage wrote *Jesus the Christ.* Some individuals may wonder if a book celebrating its first century retains its relevance. Few books written a hundred or more years ago, excepting the scriptures, are still read and enjoyed today. Those that remain highly prized are classics. *Jesus the Christ,* written at a specific time and in a specific context, is, indeed, a Latter-day Saint classic. For today's readers of this classic, modern helps assist in understanding and appreciating Elder Talmage's inspiration.

LANGUAGE

Elder Talmage's command of the English language is legendary. Throughout the book, he uses words that may require the use of a dictionary. Interestingly, Elder Talmage did not use an English-language dictionary himself as he composed *Jesus the Christ.* According to his son, Elder Talmage used only words that he completely understood and used in his own speech. John Talmage remembered:

Father was scrupulously careful in his selection of words, and it is certain that whatever word he employed would have accurately and modestly expressed his true feeling. . . . In connection with his choice of words, it may be pertinent at this point to note that in writing *Jesus the Christ*—or any others of his books, for that matter— Dr. Talmage did not refer to a dictionary. . . . Father felt that he should not use in formal writing any word of whose precise meaning he was not absolutely certain. If he needed to check the dictionary concerning any word, he felt he was not sufficiently master of it to trust himself to use it precisely as it should be used. . . . He used the dictionary frequently and thoroughly all his life, but not as a means of seeking new words when he was writing for publication. ("Assignment," 808–9.)

Elder Talmage's writing reflects some of the flowery style that was characteristic of the last half of the nineteenth century. His writing style, along with his rich vocabulary and the fact that the work contains more than eight hundred printed pages, can seem daunting. Nonetheless, we believe that a careful and full reading is worth whatever effort may be required. Study of this classic work, written in the Salt Lake Temple under the direction of the First Presidency of the Church, will provide an opportunity not only to appreciate Elder Talmage's contributions to Latter-day Saint literature but also to ponder the most important story of all time, the life of Jesus the Christ.

NEW DISCOVERIES, REVELATION, AND ADVANCES

Since 1915, new discoveries, revelation, and advances have come forth, bringing the first century and Christ's ministry into better focus. For example, Elder Talmage wrote about Capernaum:

"The exact site of the city is at present unknown" (153). The site had been identified in 1868 by British army officer and explorer Charles Wilson at the existing town of Capernaum, but scholars argued whether the true location of ancient Capernaum had actually been found. As a result, Elder Talmage noted, "We shall probably never be able to know the exact fact" (187).

Since 1915, however, additional evidence has been unearthed, and the site is no longer in dispute. Largely because of a series of excavations in Capernaum that were begun in 1968, many first-century streets, courtyards, and homes have been uncovered, including one identified as Peter's house. Scholars now agree that Capernaum has correctly been identified. Other archaeological and textual discoveries have shed light on the first century, and they not only add to the earlier understanding but also, in some cases, alter it.

Elder Talmage relied on geographical and topographical descriptions in the sources he studied as he attempted to provide accuracy to the stories he discussed. Since 1915, our knowledge of the land has greatly expanded, and in many cases we can now be much more precise about geography. For example, early in the twentieth century it was believed that the straight-line distance from Jericho to Jerusalem was a little less than fifteen miles. Modern instruments and more complete surveys indicate that the distance is seventeen miles. That is a small difference, to be sure, but it illustrates that we are continuing to learn in more detail about the land where Jesus walked.

The remarkable discovery of the Dead Sea Scrolls, beginning in 1947, helps us understand the religious world of Jesus Christ more fully than ever before. Eleven caves located on the northwestern shore of the Dead Sea have yielded the oldest known copies of all the books of the Old Testament except Esther. Along with many textual discoveries, the Dead Sea Scrolls have revealed the dynamic and innovative religious world that existed just before and during the life of Jesus Christ.

In addition to archaeological and textual discoveries, we now are blessed with access to Joseph Smith's inspired translation of the Bible. Elder Talmage did not use the Joseph Smith Translation (JST) beyond the material also found in the book of Moses in the Pearl of Great Price (JST Genesis 1 through Genesis 8:18). At the time he was writing *Jesus the Christ,* The Church of Jesus Christ of Latter-day Saints did not use the printed edition of Joseph Smith's translation, titled *Holy Scriptures: Inspired Version* and published by the Reorganized Church of Jesus Christ of Latter Day Saints (RLDS). The principal reason was that at the time no official or member of The Church of Jesus Christ of Latter-day Saints had been allowed to examine the original JST manuscripts to verify that the *Inspired Version* reflected them accurately. President Joseph F. Smith, then a member of the Quorum of the Twelve Apostles, attempted to do so during a visit with Joseph Smith III, president of the RLDS Church. Instead of being allowed to see the original manuscripts, however, President Smith was given a copy of the published *Inspired Version.*

Beginning in the 1960s, the RLDS Church began providing access to the original manuscripts of the Prophet's inspired translation, which gave LDS scholars an opportunity to compare the manuscripts with the printed *Inspired Version.* Since then, LDS writers and scholars have used the *Inspired Version* regularly in official LDS Church publications, including the footnotes and appendix of the LDS edition of the King James Version of the Bible.

Another significant advance occurred when Brigham Young University was asked to assist in conserving the original JST manuscripts. These efforts yielded important advances in our understanding of Joseph Smith's inspired work. Better transcriptions of the JST manuscripts have been created, allowing us to get even closer to the Prophet's original intent than the *Inspired Version* permitted.

Since 1915, remarkable advances in our understanding of and access to Joseph Smith's sermons and teachings on key New Testament topics provide modern prophetic commentary on the scriptures. Elder Talmage had access to some of Joseph Smith's edited sermons, as published in Franklin D. Richards and James A. Little's *A Compendium of the Doctrines of the Gospel,* published in 1882 (see, for example, 150) and B. H. Roberts's *History of the Church,* published in 1902 (see, for example, 763n*a*). We now know that these early attempts to capture the words of Joseph Smith were sometimes flawed because those who collected and published them did not always rely on primary sources and made assumptions about the authorship of some items without carefully examining the original documents.

The effort to carefully collect and publish Joseph Smith's teachings based on original and primary sources began in the late 1970s. The Joseph Smith Papers Project is making significant discoveries that will affect our understanding of Joseph Smith's teachings and help us to better understand the mission of Jesus Christ.

Elder Talmage often provides a 1915 monetary equivalent to sums mentioned in the New Testament (for example, see 517n*z*). One hundred years of inflation since *Jesus the Christ* was published have made those calculations outdated, and, as a result, new calculations are necessary to help us understand Elder Talmage's efforts to make the New Testament story meaningful to modern readers.

Another significant advance is our understanding of the nature of rabbinic writings, including the Mishnah and Talmud.

Scholars now recognize that they often represent an idealized picture of Jewish customs and laws from the perspective of later rabbis after the end of Second Temple Judaism (post–first century) and therefore do not always represent the historical reality of the first century.

Scholars today are also much more interested in preserving the individual voices of the four Gospel writers and less in providing a harmony of them, as earlier generations of scholars did. This effort to understand each Gospel as a separate and important source has heightened our appreciation for each Gospel author's individual contributions and insights.

Finally, an example of modern revelation that helps us better appreciate Jesus Christ's ministry is the vision of the redemption of the dead (Doctrine and Covenants 138), which was received by Church President Joseph F. Smith three years after *Jesus the Christ* was published. President Smith's 1918 vision greatly expands our understanding of the Savior's ministry in the spirit world between His death on the cross Friday afternoon and His Resurrection sometime early on Sunday morning.

Elder Talmage was blessed with an inquisitive nature and a conviction that truth can be discovered "by study and also by faith" (Doctrine and Covenants 88:118). If he could prepare a revised edition of *Jesus the Christ* today, he most certainly would take full advantage of the discoveries, revelation, and advances made during the last one hundred years—just as he did with some of the later editions of the book published in his lifetime when he adapted and added new notes and other content. In the preface of the third edition, prepared in March 1916, Elder Talmage noted: "The second edition of this work, consisting of ten thousand copies, appeared in December, 1915. The present or third edition presents several minor alterations in wording, and contains additional references and notes" (iv). For an example of an addition, see his inclusion of a 5 February 1916 First Presidency statement that clarifies a question about the Holy Ghost (720).

As we noted earlier, Elder Talmage's *Jesus the Christ* is often a starting point for Latter-day Saints in their own study of the life and ministry of Jesus Christ. From this beginning, students and scholars may take advantage of new revelation and research to build upon the foundation laid by Elder Talmage.

Notwithstanding discoveries made in the last century about the first-century world of Jesus Christ and textual advances regarding the New Testament, Elder Talmage's apostolic witness and testimony remain the same. We see farther today because we stand on the shoulders of giants.

A FINAL CONSIDERATION

At general conferences of The Church of Jesus Christ of Latter-day Saints, including general priesthood sessions and general women's meetings, prophets, apostles, and other Church leaders call Latter-day Saints to repentance and encourage them to make and keep sacred covenants. Their counsel is understandable to insiders, members of the Church. Outsiders, however, may come to wrong conclusions if they misunderstand the context of prophetic warnings, advice, and counsel.

Likewise, we may ourselves be outsiders as we read the New Testament. When Jesus, John the Baptist, and the Apostles called Jews, including the Pharisees, to repentance and admonished more faithful dedication to the Lord and His commandments, they were insiders having an internal conversation with their own people—the chosen people of God.

We, being from mostly Gentile nations, separated geographically from the Jews in the Holy Land and in time by more than

two thousand years, must be careful not to fall into the trap identified in the parable of the Pharisee and the publican. We must
not pray, "I thank thee, that I am not as other men are, extortion-
ers, unjust, adulterers, or even as [these Jews or Pharisees]" (Luke
18:11). Stories preserved in scripture teach us about human nature and are not intended to justify judging a specific people at a
specific time.

The stories preserved in the New Testament live in us as we
personalize them—as we liken them to ourselves, seeing ourselves
in the place of each character who is mentioned (1 Nephi 19:23).

We might become more like Jesus the Christ if we ask ourselves the following questions and carefully ponder the answers:

- Have I acted like the disciples who ran away from the Lord?
  (Mark 14:50).
- Have I behaved like the rich young ruler, more concerned
  about my personal possessions than with sharing? (Matthew
  19:22).
- Have I, like James and John, been worried about position
  and honors? (Mark 10:37).
- Have I, like the disciples in Capernaum, been offended at
  Jesus's words? (John 6:66).
- Have I, like the early disciples, failed to understand what
  Jesus was trying to teach? (Luke 9:45).
- Have I been believing, like Mary, who was blessed for her
  belief? (Luke 1:42, 45).
- Have I, like the Samaritan leper, shown gratitude to the
  Lord when He blessed me? (Luke 17:15–17).
- Has my trust in God been like that of the unnamed Gentile
  woman, to whom the Lord said, "O woman, great is thy
  faith"? (Matthew 15:28).

- Have I, like Peter, testified of Christ and then received the Lord's response, "Blessed art thou"? (Matthew 16:17).
- Have I, like James and John, responded to the Lord's call, "Come ye after me, and I will make you to become fishers of men"? (Mark 1:17).

ORGANIZATION OF THIS STUDY GUIDE

Each chapter of *Jesus the Christ* is discussed separately, and information under specific headings enables you to get the most out of your reading of Elder Talmage's most important book. Not every subhead appears in every chapter, however. Occasionally, when we had no new material for one or more of the following sections, we omitted them.

Overview. One, two, or three topics from each chapter are identified, but not every topic in each chapter is discussed.

Since 1915. Some of the most important insights based on discoveries and advances made in New Testament studies and modern revelation received since *Jesus the Christ* was first published in 1915 are highlighted.

Joseph Smith's Teachings. Extracts from Joseph Smith's sermons and writings that provide additional insights into the life, ministry, and teachings of Jesus Christ are presented. Spelling and punctuation have been modernized and paragraphing altered for easier reading, and, where appropriate, specific scripture references are noted.

Joseph Smith Translation. Quotations from the Prophet's inspired translation of the King James Version of the Bible (KJV) are included in this study guide. Extracts from that inspired translation are cited as Joseph Smith Translation (JST) in the footnotes and appendix of the LDS edition of the KJV, both print and electronic versions. The numbering of JST chapters and verses in the

LDS edition of the KJV is based on the numbering in the edition of Joseph Smith's inspired translation published by the RLDS Church (now Community of Christ) as *Holy Scriptures: Inspired Version* (Independence, MO: Herald House, 1944).

Continued work on the original JST manuscripts since the publication of the LDS edition of the KJV in 1979 has helped approximate more closely the intent of the Prophet's efforts and thus allows a more accurate text of numerous passages. As a result, we have cited JST quotations to Thomas Wayment's *Complete Joseph Smith Translation of the New Testament,* which reflects recent research and indicates the precise verse in the KJV that the Prophet changed.

Readers who would like to refer directly to the JST text may consult the footnotes in the LDS edition of the KJV to find the location of the corresponding JST passages. For example, on page 40 of this study guide, a reference to the Prophet's inspired translation has the following citation: "(JST Matthew 2:2; italics indicate changes to the KJV text)." To find the JST text in the LDS edition of the KJV, readers would go to Matthew 2:2 and consult footnote 2*a*, which reads: "JST Matt 3:2 Where is *the child* that is born, *the Messiah* of the Jews? . . ." Another example, from page 44 of this study guide, references a longer JST passage as follows: "(JST Matthew 2:23; italics indicate changes to the KJV text)." Readers would turn to Matthew 2:23 in the LDS edition of the KJV and consult footnote 23*c*, which reads: "JST Matt. 3:24–26 (Appendix)." They would then turn to the appendix in the LDS edition of the KJV where, under the heading of Matthew 3:24–26, they would find the text of the Prophet's inspired translation.

Study Questions. Each chapter ends with fact-based, thought-based, and personal application questions, some of which have been adapted from study guides for *Jesus the Christ* published in 1916, 1963, and 1963–64 (see "Selected Sources").

Glossary. This study guide contains the definitions of important theological terms and other words that may be unfamiliar to readers today. Such terms are arranged alphabetically in the glossary at the end of this guide. Use of an English-language dictionary may also be helpful.

CHAPTER 1

INTRODUCTION

In the opening chapter of *Jesus the Christ,* Elder James E. Talmage establishes the purpose of the book—namely, to understand the centrality of Christ in the Father's loving plan of salvation. In doing so, he affirms seven truths about Jesus Christ, which are touched upon in each chapter, mostly in subtle ways but at times directly and forcefully. In Elder Talmage's words, the seven truths are as follows:

1. The unity and continuity of His mission in all ages—this of necessity involving the verity of His preexistence and foreordination.
2. The fact of His antemortal Godship.
3. The actuality of His birth in the flesh as the natural issue of divine and mortal parentage.
4. The reality of His death and physical resurrection, as a result of which the power of death shall be eventually overcome.

5. The literalness of the atonement wrought by Him, including the absolute requirement of individual compliance with the laws and ordinances of His gospel as the means by which salvation may be attained.

6. The restoration of His Priesthood and the reestablishment of His Church in the current age, which is [known as] the Dispensation of the Fulness of Times.

7. The certainty of His return to earth in the near future, with power and great glory, to reign in Person and bodily presence as Lord and King. (5)

As you read *Jesus the Christ,* keep those seven truths in mind. They will allow you to see the big picture as Elder Talmage provides insights, reflections, and testimony, like one stone upon another, building a beautiful house of faith in the divinity of the "Son of the Living God, the Redeemer and Savior of the human race, the Eternal Judge of the souls of men, the Chosen and Anointed of the Father—in short, the Christ" (1–2).

It is valuable to consider that Elder Talmage did not state that one of his goals was to write a biography of Jesus of Nazareth. Instead, Elder Talmage was interested in finding the continuity in God's purpose from Adam through the Old Testament prophets, to the Nephites, to the New Testament Twelve Apostles, and through the Restoration. In other words, he set out to prepare a sacred witness of Jesus Christ, not a traditional modern biography. For this reason, there was value in Elder Talmage's study of Protestant New Testament scholarship as a foundation for the historical setting of the story. To establish the foundation for the doctrinal witness and testimony of Jesus the Christ, however, the story relied almost exclusively on the revelations of the Restoration.

After this short introduction, Elder Talmage discusses Jesus

Christ's foreordination and calling in the premortal life, the need for a Redeemer, Christ's premortal Godship, and the prophecies regarding His birth, ministry, death, and resurrection (chapters 2 through 5).

Since 1915

Jesus Christ. The name Jesus Christ may appear to be a first and a last name, but in the first century, Jews typically had only a first name. To distinguish one person with a common name from another with the same name, people were known in the first century AD by nicknames or descriptive statements, such as a unique physical attribute, their father's name, or their occupation—for example, Simon the leper (Mark 14:3), Simon Bar-jona ("Simon son of Jonah," Matthew 16:17), or Simon a tanner (Acts 10:6).

Jesus was actually named "Joshua," a common name in the first century. *Jesus* is the Greek equivalent of the Hebrew/ Aramaic name *Yeshua,* a contraction of two Hebrew words that mean "Jehovah is salvation" or "Jehovah saves." Because the New Testament was preserved in Greek, *Yeshua* became the English *Jesus* or German *Jesu* or Spanish *Jesús.*

To distinguish Jesus from the many others who had the same name, He was often referred to as Jesus of Nazareth, or Jesus from the city of Nazareth (Matthew 21:11). He was also referred to as Jesus the Christ or, in the shortened form, Jesus Christ.

The second element, *Christ,* is a title meaning "the Messiah." The Hebrew word *Messiah* was pronounced as *mashiach,* but translated into Greek, it becomes *christos.* Both of these terms mean "anointed." Thus, Jesus was known as Jesus the Anointed One (Matthew 1:1).

Chronological order of the Gospels. Three of the Gospels, Matthew, Mark, and Luke, share approximately 90 percent of their material. They are often called the synoptic Gospels, from the Greek word meaning "viewed together" or "they saw the same things." The Gospel of John, on the other hand, records many events that are not found in the synoptic Gospels and emphasizes different portions of Christ's mortal ministry. Modern readers often have a difficult time understanding the historical order of the events in Jesus's life because sometimes four different accounts of an event are given and because each of them occurs in a different position in the Gospels. These differences are largely the result of the fact that stories from Jesus's life were passed on orally before they were written down. In some instances, decades may have elapsed before the events were recorded. New Testament authors were often more interested in themes and concepts rather than chronological precision.

Often, the time when an event occurred was not as important as the event itself. It is human nature to forget the exact order of events. Today, we can consult a number of Gospel harmonies that put Gospel events into a single account to create a single historical chronology for the life of Jesus. These harmonies are based on differing assumptions and suppositions. In the 2013 Latter-day Saint edition of the Bible is a harmony of the Gospels (Appendix, 759–74) that largely favors the order of events as presented in the Gospel of Mark, which many scholars consider to be the first written Gospel account. Elder Talmage's work is based on the chronological order outlined in Frederic Farrar's *Life of Christ.*

Lifespan of Jesus. We do not know precisely how old Jesus was when He began His ministry or precisely how long His mortal ministry lasted. Traditionally, however, we assume for Him a lifespan of about thirty-three years and a three-year ministry. The evidence for this assumption derives from several sources.

The Gospel of Luke provides the only reference to an approximate age for Jesus at the start of His ministry: "And Jesus himself began to be about thirty years of age" (Luke 3:23), reminding readers of the age of priestly service mentioned in Leviticus. Following Luke's approximation that Jesus was about thirty years old when His mortal ministry began, scholars then count the number of Passover celebrations that occurred during His ministry and estimate the length of the ministry. In Matthew, Mark, and Luke, however, only one specific mention of the Passover is made (Matthew 26:2); therefore, we could surmise that the ministry lasted only a year.

The Gospel of John, however, mentions at least two Passover feasts and possibly three (John 6:4; 11:55). The third Passover may be intended in John 5:1, which refers to an otherwise unnamed feast, possibly Passover, or perhaps the Feast of Tabernacles.

Adding these two pieces of evidence together—Luke's claim that Jesus was about thirty years old when He began His ministry and John's claim that the ministry continued for three to four years—suggests that Jesus was about thirty-three or thirty-four years old at the time of His death.

The Book of Mormon seems to corroborate this evidence: "And it came to pass in the thirty and fourth year, in the first month, on the fourth day of the month, there arose a great storm, such an one as never had been known in all the land" (3 Nephi 8:5). This chapter places the calamities that took place among the Nephites at the time of Christ's death about thirty-four years after His birth. Limiting this evidence is the fact that the length of a Nephite/Lamanite year is not known; indeed, various societies intend different lengths of time when using the term *year*.

Joseph Smith's Teachings

1 Corinthians 15:3–4. "The fundamental principles of our religion are the testimony of the apostles and prophets concerning Jesus Christ, 'that he died, was buried, and rose again the third day, and ascended up into heaven;' and all other things are only appendages to these, which pertain to our religion" ("In Obedience to Our Promise," *Elders' Journal,* July 1838, 44, as cited in Jackson, *Joseph Smith's Commentary,* 167).

Joseph Smith Translation

The Joseph Smith Translation, including the material in the book of Moses, connects the will of the Father with the work of the Son. That plan was, according to the JST, equally eternal with God—or, in other words, in the beginning with God (JST John 1:1–3). This perspective helps close the gap between the Old and New Testaments and helps readers see how these two important witnesses share a common goal, that of extending the blessings of the gospel to all who will accept it and embrace it.

Study Questions

1. What sources in addition to the Bible are available to Latter-day Saints to learn more about Jesus Christ? What is one additional insight from each source that is not explicitly preserved in the Bible?
2. How is Jesus Christ central to the Father's plan?
3. How do you feel when you use "the sacred name of Jesus Christ" when you pray, give a talk, or administer a blessing (5)?

CHAPTER 2

PREEXISTENCE AND FOREORDINATION OF THE CHRIST

In the second chapter of *Jesus the Christ*, the topic of the war in heaven is treated in some detail. That information is absolutely essential for the reader to fully understand the need for a Redeemer. The scriptural foundation for teachings about the war in heaven is found in the book of Revelation: "And there was war in heaven: Michael and his angels fought against the dragon; and the dragon fought and his angels" (Revelation 12:7).

The Restoration expands our understanding of the premortal world as it is taught in the Old and New Testaments. The war between Michael and Satan is described in greater detail in the book of Moses, and in a revelation now recorded as Abraham 3, we learn the details of that conflict:

> And there stood one among them that was like unto God, and he said unto those who were with him: We will go down, for there is space there, and we will take of these materials, and we will make an earth whereon

these may dwell; and we will prove them herewith, to see if they will do all things whatsoever the Lord their God shall command them; and they who keep their first estate shall be added upon; and they who keep not their first estate shall not have glory in the same kingdom with those who keep their first estate; and they who keep their second estate shall have glory added upon their heads for ever and ever. And the Lord said: Whom shall I send? And one answered like unto the Son of Man: Here am I, send me. And another answered and said: Here am I, send me. And the Lord said: I will send the first. And the second was angry, and kept not his first estate; and, at that day, many followed after him. (Abraham 3:24–28)

After the war in heaven, the need for a Redeemer became obvious—namely, our need for someone who not only could redeem us from the Fall but who would also offer to us a perfect example—God's divine Son, who could guide us on the path of salvation. Those who lost the war in heaven and were cast out attempt to hinder our way back to God. Not only does Jesus Christ show us the path back to the Father and encourage us to follow Him but He also provides the means by which we will return to the presence of God: "Jesus saith unto him, I am the way, the truth, and the life: no man cometh unto the Father, but by me" (John 14:6).

SINCE 1915

Premortal life. The doctrine of the premortal life is taught sparingly in the Bible, but it is an important foundation for understanding Jesus Christ and what He came to earth to accomplish. Perhaps the most specific mention of the premortality of Christ in the Bible comes in the opening lines of the Gospel of

John: "In the beginning was the Word, and the Word was with God, and the Word was God. The same was in the beginning with God" (John 1:1–2; see also vv. 3–5).

The doctrine of premortality is also highlighted in passages such as John 9:1–2: "And as Jesus passed by, he saw a man which was blind from his birth. And his disciples asked him, saying, Master, who did sin, this man, or his parents, that he was born blind?" The story implies that the disciples believed an individual was born without sight because of sins committed prior to his birth, although the story does not specifically mention that fact, and Jesus points out that the disciples were incorrect in their assumptions about the man's blindness being the result of his own or his parents' sins.

Genesis and the book of Moses. The book of Moses is an extract from the Joseph Smith Translation of Genesis. Although Moses 1 has no counterpart in the book of Genesis (it is a new revelation), Moses 2–7 represents the material found in JST Genesis 1–6. The book of Moses, along with the book of Abraham, is the foundation of the doctrines taught in the first six chapters of *Jesus the Christ*. To understand more fully what Elder Talmage intended in these opening chapters, study the book of Moses and the book of Abraham, where such doctrines as the premortality of men and women, the divine council in heaven, and the plan of salvation are discussed in detail.

The Book of Mormon testifies of Christ. The Book of Mormon provides a key witness to the importance of Jesus Christ and His ministry in extending the blessings of the Father's plan of salvation to all the sons and daughters of God. Specifically, the Book of Mormon records the visit of the resurrected Christ to the Nephites (3 Nephi 11–27) and teaches about the importance of His mission (2 Nephi 11). In its fullest sense, the Book of Mormon is, indeed, "Another Testament of Jesus Christ." As used in the New Testament, *testament* has the primary meaning of "covenant." During the Last Supper, Jesus taught, "This cup is the new testament in my blood, which is shed for you" (Luke 22:20). He was referring to a new covenant because of His atoning blood—namely, the sacrament. The Book of Mormon is another covenant of Jesus Christ because it testifies of the covenant that was extended to the people of Nephi.

Joseph Smith's Teachings

Genesis 1:26–28. "At the first organization in heaven, we were all present and saw the Savior chosen and appointed, and the plan of salvation made and we sanctioned it. We came to this earth that we might have a body and present it pure before God in the Celestial kingdom" (Discourse, 5 January 1841, reported by William Clayton, The Joseph Smith Papers, accessed 21 February 2014, http://josephsmithpapers.org/paperSummary /discourse-5-january-1841-as-reported-by-william-clayton?p=4).

"Jesus contended that there would be certain souls that would be condemned, and the Devil said he could save them all. As the Grand Council gave in for Jesus Christ, so the Devil fell and all who put up their heads for him" (Discourse, 7 April 1844, recorded by Thomas Bullock, as cited in Jackson, *Joseph Smith's Commentary,* 13; see also Ehat and Cook, *Words of Joseph Smith,* 353).

Joseph Smith Translation

The changes the Prophet Joseph Smith made to the opening verses of the Gospel of John highlight the premortal ministry of the Lord and His part in proclaiming the plan of salvation: "In the beginning was the *gospel preached through the Son. And the gospel was the* Word, and the Word was with *the Son, and the Son was with God,* and the *Son* was *of* God" (JST John 1:1; see also vv. 2–18; italics indicate changes to the KJV text). These changes connect the mortal ministry with the premortal ministry of Christ and underscore many of the teachings in the first chapters of *Jesus the Christ.* They help us see that the plan of salvation is coeternal with God the Father and His Son Jesus Christ.

STUDY QUESTIONS

1. In what way does knowledge of the pre-earth life provide perspective on mortality?

2. One of the most explicit witnesses of Christ's premortality is found in John 1:1–18. What do these verses teach concerning Jesus Christ's role in Heavenly Father's plan?

3. What blessings flow from agency? What consequences flow from the misuse of agency?

CHAPTER 3

THE NEED OF
A REDEEMER

Elder Talmage begins chapter 3 by stating, "The entire human race existed as spirit-beings in the primeval world, and . . . they were endowed with the powers of agency or choice while yet but spirits" (17). He then discusses the question of how God's omnipotence (possessing all power) relates to agency and also provides an answer to the underlying question of how we are able to exercise agency even though God knows all things. Elder Talmage believes that God's knowledge of all things (His omniscience) does not infringe upon our ability to make choices. Instead, as our knowledge grows in harmony with the will of God, His knowledge of things can guide and direct us in our quest for perfection. Elder Talmage affirms the divine truth that God knows all things: "I *know* their works and their thoughts" (Isaiah 66:18; emphasis added).

In discussing the need for a Redeemer and one who could offer a perfect sacrifice, Elder Talmage focuses on three key reasons why Jesus was uniquely qualified to atone for the sins of human-kind: Jesus was (1) "the one and only sinless Man," (2) "the Only Begotten of the Father and therefore the only Being born to earth possessing in their fulness the attributes of both Godhood and manhood," and (3) "the One who had been chosen in the heavens and foreordained to this service" (21).

SINCE 1915

Agency. Note that Elder Talmage, like most members of the Church of that day, uses "free agency" when discussing the ability to choose (134). In 2009, Elder D. Todd Christofferson offered a helpful fine-tuning of this principle: "In years past we generally used the term *free agency*. . . . More recently we have taken note that *free agency* does not appear in the scriptures. They talk of our being 'free to choose' and 'free to act' for ourselves (2 Nephi 2:27; 10:23; see also Helaman 14:30) and of our obligation to do many things of our own 'free will' (D&C 58:27). But the word *agency* appears either by itself or with the modifier *moral:* 'That every man may act in doctrine and principle . . . according to the *moral agency* which I have given unto him, that every man may be accountable for his own sins in the day of judgment' (D&C 101:78; emphasis added)" ("Moral Agency," *Ensign,* June 2009, 47).

Eve. Elder Talmage speaks of Eve in a way that could imply she had little or no understanding of the consequences of her actions and her role in the plan of salvation, although he also adds, "It is not proposed to consider here at length the doctrine of the fall" (19). More recently, Elder Dallin H. Oaks offered this testimony of Eve's role in the plan of salvation: "Some Christians condemn Eve for her act, concluding that she and her daughters are somehow flawed by it. Not the Latter-day Saints! Informed by revelation, we celebrate Eve's act and honor her wisdom and courage in the great episode called the Fall." Elder Oaks further quoted the words of President Joseph Fielding Smith: "'I never speak of the part Eve took in this fall as a sin, nor do I accuse Adam of a sin. . . . This was a transgression of the law, but not a sin . . . for it was something that Adam and Eve had to do!'" (Oaks, "The Great Plan of Happiness," *Ensign,* November 1993, 73; Joseph Fielding Smith, *Doctrines of Salvation,* comp. Bruce R. McConkie, 3 vols., Salt Lake City: Bookcraft, 1954–56, 1:114–15).

JOSEPH SMITH'S TEACHINGS

Abraham's writings. "[An] Everlasting covenant was made between three personages before the organization of this earth and relates to their dispensation of things to men on the earth. These personages according to Abraham's record are God the first, the Creator; God the second, the Redeemer; and God the third, the Witness or Testator" ("Extracts from Wm Clayton's Private Book," 9 March 1841, 10–11, L. John Nuttall Collection, L. Tom Perry Special Collections, Harold B. Lee Library, Brigham Young University, Provo, Utah, as cited in Ehat and Cook, *Words of Joseph Smith,* 87–88).

JOSEPH SMITH TRANSLATION

Foremost among the changes made in the Joseph Smith Translation are those made to John 5:29 and the manner in which those changes laid the foundation for the revelation of Doctrine and Covenants 76, known as the vision of the three degrees of glory. The important contribution of the JST in this regard is both textual and procedural—it reminds us how intimately connected scripture study is to revelation and how seeing a few words in a different light can open up new insights. On 16 February

1832, the Prophet Joseph Smith and Sidney Rigdon were translating the New Testament together. They came upon the peculiar wording of John 5:29 that mentions two resurrections: "the resurrection of life" and "the resurrection of damnation." We cannot possibly know or say what they felt in those moments, but the two phrases from this verse caught their attention.

In his revision of this verse, the Prophet changed the wording to read, "And shall come forth; they *who* have done good, *in* the resurrection of *the just;* and they *who* have done evil, *in* the resurrection of *the unjust; and shall all be judged of the Son of Man*" (JST John 5:29; italics indicate changes to the KJV text). As a result of Joseph's and Sidney's meditating upon the change for John 5:29, one of the most majestic views of heaven that has ever been recorded was received (Doctrine and Covenants 76). In section 76, we learn of the fall of Satan and his opposition to the plan of salvation, of the premortal council in heaven, and of the eternal glory that awaits the faithful (Doctrine and Covenants 76:28, 39–40).

Another recent discovery deals with the original JST manuscript reading of a passage found in the current printed edition of the book of Moses: "In the Garden of Eden, gave I unto man his agency" (Moses 7:32). The original manuscript represents more accurately Joseph Smith's revelation: "And in the Garden of Eden, man had agency" (Manuscript Text Moses 7:32; Jackson, *Book of Moses,* 166). This insight makes it clear, as Elder Talmage states, that the spirit beings "were endowed with the powers of agency or choice while yet but spirits" (17).

STUDY QUESTIONS

1. What is sin? What was Adam and Eve's transgression? How have the fall of Adam and Eve and its consequences been a blessing to the sons and daughters of God?

2. Elder Talmage notes three distinct reasons why Jesus Christ was uniquely qualified to be the Redeemer of the world. What are those reasons, and what scriptures support these truths?

3. How can you appreciate Jesus's unique role as Savior and Redeemer more fully this week?

THE ANTEMORTAL GODSHIP OF CHRIST

Based on his earlier work *The Articles of Faith* (1899), chapter 4 of *Jesus the Christ* teaches about the Godhead. Elder Talmage states that the Godhead is composed of "(1) God the Eternal Father, (2) His Son Jesus Christ, and (3) the Holy Ghost" (32). The doctrine of the Godhead is founded upon the revelation recorded in modern Restoration scripture: "The Father has a body of flesh and bones as tangible as man's; the Son also; but the Holy Ghost has not a body of flesh and bones, but is a personage of Spirit. Were it not so, the Holy Ghost could not dwell in us. A man may receive the Holy Ghost, and it may descend upon him and not tarry with him" (Doctrine and Covenants 130:22–23).

Latter-day Saint doctrine teaches that God the Father and God the Son are related literally and are completely united in purpose, but they remain separate and distinct beings. In understanding their unique relationship, we need only visualize God in heaven directing and inspiring the actions of His Son on the earth.

Using Restoration scripture and the Old and New Testaments, Elder Talmage demonstrates that the Father, the Son, and the Holy Ghost are one in purpose, yet distinct and separate beings. Early Christians were pressed to explain how the God of the Old Testament and the God of the New Testament, who seemed so different to many, were united in purpose. Additionally, those same Christians were troubled by the idea of a material or physical deity, so they sought to redefine God as eternal but immaterial. Western (Roman Catholic and Protestant) and Eastern Orthodox Christianity differ on how to answer such questions, but one of the results of those discussions was an emphasis on the eternal immaterial unity of God (the Father and the Son), regardless of who was being spoken of.

In attempting to understand the full scope of the Son's part in the Father's plan of salvation for all His children, we should realize how broadly our loving Heavenly Father conceived salvation. Salvation cannot be limited in any way, for all are invited to come unto Him (see 2 Nephi 26:33); that is, not a single person will be left out from the opportunity to be saved. Elder Talmage testifies that the Father's purpose is fully realized in the mission of the Son, and these truths are part of an introduction to the study of the life of Christ.

SINCE 1915

Trinity. Although Elder Talmage uses the expression "Holy Trinity" (see, for example, 32), he does not use it in the same way Protestants and Catholics typically do.

"Doctrinal Exposition" (1916). Not long after *Jesus the Christ* was released in 1915, the First Presidency and the Quorum of the Twelve Apostles issued an important statement entitled "The Father and the Son: A Doctrinal Exposition of the First Presidency and Twelve" (*Improvement Era,* August 1916, 934–42). Representing the united voice of the First Presidency and the Quorum of the Twelve, the document provides Church members a simple explanation of the relationships between the Father and the Son and the use of "Father" in the scriptures when it refers to Deity.

JOSEPH SMITH'S TEACHINGS

John 17:9–11. "'That we might be one,' or to say, 'be of one mind in the unity of the faith.' But everyone [is] a different or separate person, and so [are] God, and Jesus Christ, and the Holy Ghost separate persons. But they all agree in one or the selfsame thing. But the Holy Ghost is yet a spiritual body and [is] waiting to take to himself a body, as the Savior did or as God did or the Gods before them took bodies" (Discourse, 16 June 1844, recorded by George Laub, as cited in Jackson, *Joseph Smith's Commentary,* 142).

"Joseph also said that the Holy Ghost is now in a state of probation which if he should perform in righteousness he may pass the same or a similar course of things that the Son has" (Franklin D. Richards, "Scriptural Items," 27 August 1843, Church History Library, The Church of Jesus Christ of Latter-day Saints, Salt Lake City, Utah).

JOSEPH SMITH TRANSLATION

An important contribution of the Joseph Smith Translation in this chapter is the emphasis it places on the doctrine of our need for a Redeemer. In changing Luke 3:4–11, the Prophet added these important words of prophecy foretelling and visualizing the ministry of Jesus Christ: "*And to be a light unto all who sit in dark-ness, unto the uttermost parts of the earth; to bring to pass the resur-rection from the dead, and to ascend up on high, to dwell on the right hand of the Father*" (JST Luke 3:4–11; italics indicate changes to the KJV text).

The changes to these verses highlight the growing interest of the Restoration in taking the gospel to all the world and in administering vicarious work for the dead. It is as if, in adding these words to the Gospel of Luke, the Prophet Joseph Smith is describing the roadmap for the Restoration of the Church in the latter days. These verses also make clear that the prophets testified of the Redeemer and of the way in which the work of redemption would be extended to all people—to Israel and to the Gentiles. That message of salvation would affect lives and would not be ful-filled until the latter days, when the gospel would be taken "unto the uttermost parts of the earth."

STUDY QUESTIONS

1. Why do we appropriately identify the Father, the Son, and the Holy Ghost as "one God"?

2. What examples are found in the scriptures of the Father in-troducing the Son?

3. How is Jesus the Father? (see also Mosiah 15:1–5).

CHAPTER 5

EARTHLY ADVENT OF THE CHRIST PREDICTED

Along with Elder Talmage's discussion about the reach and extent of the Son's ministry is the need for a discussion about the apparent discrepancies between the Old and New Testaments. The differences in tone and content between the two testaments of the Bible are easily perceived. The Old Testament was originally written in Hebrew, with some material preserved in Aramaic, resulting in various names and spellings. Additionally, the Old Testament is filled with animal sacrifices, sacred holidays, and special religious ceremonies and practices that are unfamiliar to the modern reader. By contrast, in the books following the Gospels in the New Testament, little mention is made of animal sacrifice; almost no emphasis is given to the Jewish feast days; God is noticeably merciful; and a new covenant replaces the old covenant.

Many things, of course, unite the two testaments of the Bible, and this short discussion cannot mention all of them. But one thing that unites the two parts most completely is the sacrifice of lambs.

In the Old Testament, the Israelites were commanded to offer sacrifices on specific occasions and for certain sins and at important milestones in life, such as birth. In many of these sacrifices, the person offering the sacrifice was required by the law of Moses to offer a lamb. These lambs were offered on specific holidays, such as Passover, and were specifically mandated in the law of Moses (Exodus 12:3–6).

To the Gospel writers, Jesus Christ was the ultimate "lamb of God," offered as the Paschal Lamb during the Passover season when He died on the cross. Apostles and prophets testified that His death had been prefigured by the offering of unblemished male lambs in the ancient temple (John 1:29; 1 Corinthians 5:7; 1 Peter 1:19). The sheep that were sacrificed as part of the law of Moses and their representation of Christ as the Lamb of God are a symbol that unifies the Testaments.

JOSEPH SMITH'S TEACHINGS

Moses 5:4–8. "The ordinance or institution of offering blood in sacrifice was only designed to be performed till Christ was offered up and shed his blood that man might look forward with faith to that time. . . . We conclude, that whenever the Lord revealed himself to men in ancient days, and commanded them to offer sacrifice to him, that it was done that they might look forward in faith to the time of his coming, and rely upon the power of that atonement for a remission of their sins. . . . We may conclude that though there were different dispensations, yet all things which God communicated to his people, were calculated to draw their minds to the great object, and to teach them to rely upon him alone as the Author of their salvation, as contained in his law" ("The Elders of the Church in Kirtland, to Their Brethren Abroad," *Evening and Morning Star,* March 1834, 143, as cited in Jackson, *Joseph Smith's Commentary,* 15).

Moses 7:62. "God clearly manifested to Enoch the redemption which he prepared by offering the Messiah as a Lamb slain from before the foundation of the world, [and] by virtue of the same the glorious resurrection of the Savior and resurrection of all the human family" ("To the Elders of the Church of Latter Day Saints," *Messenger and Advocate,* November 1835, 209).

JOSEPH SMITH TRANSLATION

In the book of Hebrews, the Joseph Smith Translation changes a verse to reflect the continuity between the purpose and practice of offering animal sacrifices. The changes in the verse are subtle, but they offer renewed emphasis to the idea that the sacrifices of the Mosaic law were intended to remove the sins of the people: "*And not as those high priests* who *offered up sacrifice* daily, first *for their own sins, and then for the sins of the people; for he needeth not [to] offer sacrifice* for his own sins, *for he knew no sins; but* for the *sins of* the *people. And* this he did once when he offered up himself*" (JST Hebrews 7:27; italics indicate changes to the KJV text).

STUDY QUESTIONS

1. Why did God tell His children, through His prophets, about the coming of His Son so many years prior to the birth of Jesus in Bethlehem?
2. Why was the ordinance of sacrifice so important?
3. How may we compare the prophecies found in the Bible and the Book of Mormon about the coming of the Messiah?

CHAPTER 6

THE MERIDIAN
OF TIME

Elder Talmage discusses in detail the setting for the birth, mortal ministry, and Crucifixion of Jesus Christ. This historically focused chapter treats important topics in ways that Elder Talmage hoped would help modern readers enter the world of first-century Judaism.

Our understanding of first-century Judaism has increased significantly since 1915 because of momentous discoveries and reevaluation of previously used sources based on those discoveries. We can compare advances made in lighting from Thomas Edison's first commercially practical light bulb in 1879 until today to advances made in our knowledge of the first century AD since Elder Talmage wrote *Jesus the Christ* in 1915.

As already noted, the important discovery of the Dead Sea Scrolls expanded our understanding of the religious landscape of the Holy Land during the first century. As a result of this and other discoveries, many scholars today speak of first-century

Judaism(s), because they no longer see Judaism as a unified, monolithic religious movement the way an earlier generation of scholars did.

For example, Elder Talmage makes occasional reference to the Jewish Mishnah (early third century AD) and Jewish Gemara (fifth or sixth centuries AD), which, combined, became the Jewish Talmud (the Palestinian Talmud dates from about the fourth century and the Babylonian Talmud dates to the fifth and sixth centuries). As an important part of the religious literature of Rabbinic Judaism, a post–New Testament development, Talmudic writings are no longer thought to be as helpful a tool for reconstruction of the religious landscape of the first century in Galilee and Judea as they were once believed to be.

Latter-day Saints need to understand that from the end of the Old Testament to the beginning of the New Testament stands a 450-year era commonly known as the intertestamental period. This long stretch of time was filled with monumental events that changed the society and character of the Holy Land. Most notably, following Malachi's death in about 450 BC, no authorized prophetic voice was heard again for almost five hundred years. Malachi's death marked the end of one dispensation, and without a prophet, the people began to divide into various parties and groups, each claiming the right to interpret the holy scriptures. God eventually sent a new prophet, John the Baptist, to begin a new dispensation. Nevertheless, like the Reformation that preceded the Restoration, the intertestamental period included events that prepared the world for the coming of Jesus Christ.

Not all inspired voices were completely stilled. Indeed, this period witnessed a remarkable time for production of religiously themed literature: the translation of the Hebrew Bible into Greek, known as the Septuagint; the beginning of the creation of the

Dead Sea Scrolls; the Apocrypha; and Apocalyptic literature. It also witnessed the development and refinement of religious ideas concerning angels, resurrection, and heaven and hell.

Each of the divisions within Judaism, such as the Sadducees, the Pharisees, and the Essenes, had its own unique beliefs and approaches to scripture that were as different as the distinct Christian denominations in existence today. Ancient Jews accepted different parts of the Old Testament as authoritative, and they held differing views on the temple and priesthood. Further, each group held different ideas about the promised Messiah (some may not have even believed in the coming of a Messiah). Yet most Jews were united by a belief in Jehovah, the authority of the Torah (the first five books of the Old Testament), the covenant of God established at Sinai, a promised land, and the Lord's temple in Jerusalem. This is the world into which God's Son was born.

Over the past one hundred years, one significant advance in our understanding of the Jewish religious landscape during the first century AD shows that Jesus was completely Jewish and very much a part of His Jewish world. For example, He used imagery and concepts familiar to those who heard His teachings, and He engaged in legal debates with other Jewish teachers. We should remember that He *was* a Jew, as were all of His early followers, and Jesus understood His world through the lens of faith in His Father, the Torah, and Israel's divine call and mission to be a "kingdom of priests, and an holy nation" (Exodus 19:6).

Nevertheless, we clearly understand from reading the Bible that Jesus Christ was different, and in some cases markedly different, from others (Mark 1:21–22, 27). His inspired teachings often contrasted with the efforts of individuals who attempted to read, understand, and apply the scriptures without His inspired insight. Isaiah prophesied about the coming Messiah: "The Spirit of the Lord God is upon me; because the Lord hath anointed me to preach good tidings unto the meek; he hath sent me to bind up the brokenhearted, to proclaim liberty to the captives, and the opening of the prisons to them that are bound; to proclaim the acceptable year of the Lord, and the day of vengeance of our God; to comfort all that mourn; to appoint unto them that mourn in Zion, to give unto them beauty for ashes, the oil of joy for mourning, the garment of praise for the spirit of heaviness; that they might be called trees of righteousness, the planting of the Lord, that he might be glorified" (Isaiah 61:1–3).

Since 1915

The Messiah. Most people today think of the Messiah as a divine figure who will descend from heaven and redeem humankind from oppression and sin. In the first century, however, Jewish Messianic expectations varied greatly—especially what he would do and when he would come. Many Jews did not believe that the Messiah would be a divine figure; rather, they thought that although he would be called by God, he would be fully human, anointed with God's Spirit, and adopted as God's son—to deliver them from their enemies (Psalm 2). During the Roman occupation of Judea and Galilee, the hope and expectation of the coming of a military king-messiah increased dramatically. Messianic expectations also included priestly figures who wanted an end to the perceived corruption in the Jerusalem temple and apocalyptic messengers based on the visions of Daniel.

When some of the followers of Jesus proclaimed Him as the Messiah, which in the New Testament is translated into the Greek term *christos,* or Christ, they were likely expressing some of these divergent beliefs. Luke 24 and Matthew 16 indicate that even the disciples did not have a clear understanding of the type of messiah

Jesus would be until after the Resurrection. Some wanted Him to rule Israel (John 6:15), and others believed in Him in ways that are probably very similar to our own (Matthew 16:16). But in calling Jesus the Christ (that is, the Messiah), His followers were expressing a profound sense of trust in Him that He would deliver them, either from sin or oppression or both.

Dead Sea Scrolls. The most important biblical archaeological discovery in the twentieth century was the Dead Sea Scrolls. Among the oldest known copies of every book in the Old Testament, except Esther, were the sectarian writings of the Essenes (see below), a group known about only from other sources, such as Josephus, a first-century Jewish historian.

Pharisees and Sadducees. The Pharisees and Sadducees are the two most prominent Jewish religious groups mentioned in the New Testament. Both arose toward the end of the intertestamental period, first attested in late second century BC. *Pharisee* may mean "set apart," which would correspond to their efforts to separate themselves from influences of the wider Hellenistic culture. They believed in angels, spirits, physical resurrection, and the oral law, which is identified as the traditions of the fathers in the New Testament (Matthew 15:2). The Sadducees were a smaller but more powerful group, representing the priestly aristocracy in Jerusalem who controlled the temple. They accepted only the five books of Moses (Torah) as authoritative texts and denied the physical resurrection. They did not follow Pharisaical tradition or protocol in their deliberations or implementation of policy. Traditionally, scholars assumed that the Essenes, Sadducees, and other priestly groups disappeared with the destruction of the Jerusalem temple in AD 70. However, recent scholarship has shown that some of these groups survived that event and continued to influence Jewish society in subsequent centuries.

Essenes and Herodians. The Essenes were an ultraconservative religious party known to us mostly from a few ancient sources such as Josephus—until the discovery of the Dead Sea Scrolls, which contained their own sacred texts. They described themselves as the "Sons of Light" and may have believed that the Jewish War against the Romans (AD 66–70) was the final battle. They focused on ritual purity and waited for a military messiah and a priestly messiah. The Herodians are generally assumed to be a political party that supported the Herodian dynasty. However, a few scholars believe that *Herodians* was a nickname for the Essenes because Herod the Great protected them against persecution by other Jewish religious groups. In the New Testament, they work with the Pharisees in attempting "to catch [Jesus] in his words" (Mark 12:13).

Sanhedrin. The word *Sanhedrin* means "gathered together" and may refer to the place of gathering. Recent scholarship has reevaluated sources in light of new discoveries, causing us to question our earlier understanding of the Sanhedrin. What we now know is that the Sanhedrin in the first century was little more than Jerusalem's city council. It had much less authority than is ascribed to it by the Mishnah, which likely represents what the rabbis wished the Sanhedrin to have been. The Sanhedrin is mentioned a number of times in the Gospels (Mark 14:55; 15:1; Luke 22:66; John 11:47; Acts 23:1ff).

Rabbi. The term *rabbi,* which first appears in the New Testament, was a term of respect used for teachers and scholars of the law of Moses. There seems to be no evidence that there were any specific requirements to qualify a person to be called a rabbi in Jewish circles during the first century. Unlike the priests who inherited their roles by birth, Torah teachers and scholars chose their roles. The term means "my master" but not in the technical sense as it was used later in Rabbinic Judaism (see below) where it became associated with a specific group who had met certain requirements, including training as well as age and marriage qualifications.

Interestingly, the King James Version (KJV) translators were not consistent in the way they translated the Greek transliteration of *rabbi* (*Ραββι*) found in the New Testament. Of the seventeen times it appears in the four Gospels, they translated it as "rabbi" only eight times. In the other instances, they translated *rabbi* as "Master," possibly revealing a Protestant bias regarding the term (see, for example, John 4:31; 9:2; 11:8).

Rabbinic Judaism, or Rabbinism. Considered a mainstream movement sometime after the sixth century AD, Rabbinic Judaism developed as a result of Judaism's loss of their temple and is simply one surviving element of Judaism's past. Rabbinic Judaism uses the Talmud, a collection of sayings dealing with Jewish law that was collected over time and finally codified in the sixth or seventh century AD. Studying this dynamic, but late, movement is less helpful in reconstructing the history and religious dynamic of the first century than it was thought to be before 1915. Recent discoveries, including the Dead Sea Scrolls in 1947, provide a more expanded picture of the religious landscape in the time of Jesus.

Politics at the time of Jesus. In the first century BC, Rome continued to expand its empire eastward into Syria, Judea, and Galilee. As in its other provinces, Rome sought to maintain peace while establishing a thriving civic infrastructure that would expand the local economy and bring additional taxes and revenues into Roman coffers. Rome prided itself on extending what they called the *pax romana,* or Roman peace, to far-flung territories. Many areas conquered by Rome benefited from the presence of large Roman armies and a less corrupt civil administration. However, most of the conquered territories lost some of their individual identity, rites, and customs. Rome was tolerant and even accepting of other religions, but locals in the provinces often sought to gain the favor of their Roman rulers by embracing Roman customs and ways.

In Judea and Galilee, as in other provinces, Rome often worked through local rulers who understood the beliefs and customs of the people. These leaders made a pact with Rome, promising to maintain order and peace to ensure that taxes and tolls continued to flow. In return, Rome promised to allow them to retain some powers and maintain their social positions.

In the case of Judea and Galilee, the Herodian family, first under Herod the Great and later under the direction of his sons and grandsons, ruled under the blessing and guidance of Rome. When Herod the Great died in 4 BC, three of his sons—Archelaus, Antipas, and Philip—began ruling portions of Herod's former dominion as separate and competing kingdoms. Archelaus was eventually deposed because of his erratic behavior and despotic tendencies. His portion of Herod the Great's kingdom was then governed by a Roman prefect sent to rule for a specified period of time. Today the best known of those governors is Pontius Pilate.

Joseph Smith's Teachings

Matthew 3:1–6. Providing greater detail to the historical context of John the Baptist's ministry at the beginning of the first century, Joseph Smith taught, "When the set time was come, John came forth. And when he took up his priesthood, he came bounding out of the wilderness, saying, 'Repent ye: for the kingdom of heaven is at hand.' He, having received the holy anointing, was the only lawful administrator, and the Jews all knew it. . . . All Jerusalem and all Judea came out to be baptized of John: Sadducees, Pharisees, Essenes" (Discourse, 23 July 1843, recorded by James Burgess, as cited in Jackson, *Joseph Smith's Commentary,* 77; see also Ehat and Cook, *Words of Joseph Smith,* 235).

JOSEPH SMITH TRANSLATION

One interesting Joseph Smith Translation change raises some questions about the personal beliefs of Herod the Great: "And when he had gathered all the chief priests and scribes of the people together, he demanded of them, *saying,* Where *is the place that is written of by the prophets in which* Christ should be born? *For he greatly feared, yet he believed not the prophets*" (JST Matthew 2:4; italics indicate changes to the KJV text). This may indicate that Herod, at the time of Jesus's birth, had adopted the Sadducean position on Bible authority, accepting only the Torah (the five books of Moses), or that he did not believe their prophecies about the coming Messiah.

STUDY QUESTIONS

1. How may we compare world conditions during Christ's ministry and today?
2. Why were there religious divisions among the Jews during the first century AD? Why are there religious divisions among Christians today?
3. What can you do to be more united in purpose with the First Presidency and the Quorum of the Twelve Apostles?

CHAPTER 7

GABRIEL'S ANNUNCIATION OF JOHN AND OF JESUS

Elder Talmage draws most of his information for chapter 7 from the Gospel of Luke, focusing on Gabriel's visit to Zacharias in the temple at Jerusalem and to Mary in Nazareth. Often, readers focus on the prophecies regarding the coming of the Messiah; however, similar prophecies were made regarding His forerunner, John the Baptist. In fact, one of the most powerful threads in the story of Jesus's birth is that God also prepared John the Baptist, who would both baptize Jesus and testify of His name. Matthew and Luke testify of this continuity in purpose and coordination in the effort to extend salvation unto all of God's children.

Later in His ministry, Jesus reflected upon the role that John played in preparing the way for Him: "There is another that beareth witness of me; and I know that the witness which he witnesseth of me is true. Ye sent unto John, and he bare witness unto the truth" (John 5:32–33). Luke and Matthew illuminate how this order of events was divinely guided and revealed through Gabriel and through parents who were prepared to raise John and Jesus.

In the Gospel of Luke, the story begins when, after a long silence, an angel of the Lord appeared in the temple to a "righteous" priest. Elder Talmage provides background and contextual information about Zacharias's labor in the temple and his remarkable experience as he fulfilled his duty as a priest. Several months later, the same angel, Gabriel, visited Mary in the small village of Nazareth in Galilee.

Addressing the theme of opposition to the young family of Jesus, Luke and Matthew narrate events that caused the family to reflect on their experiences. Luke notes the concern Mary may have felt in being pregnant before her marriage to Joseph: "And Mary arose in those days, and went into the hill country with *haste,* into a city of Juda" (Luke 1:39; emphasis added). He also notes on several occasions that "Mary kept all these things, *and pondered them in her heart*" (Luke 2:19; emphasis added). It seems that Luke felt that a story needed to be told about the difficulties the family faced. In Luke, even more than in Matthew, the opposition surrounding the birth of Jesus is told in a very personal way—a mother who may be ostracized, a mother carrying the weight of knowing her son's calling.

SINCE 1915

The genealogies of Jesus. Two genealogies for Jesus are preserved in the New Testament, one in Matthew and the other in Luke. Various attempts have been made to understand these records, including the proposition that one represents the genealogy of Joseph and the other the genealogy of Mary. Scholars have surmised that the differences between them are related to purpose: Matthew highlights Jesus's descent from Abraham, making Him part of Israel's heritage. Luke highlights Jesus's descent from Adam, making Him part of the entire human family. Without additional information or revelation, we cannot sort out all the issues. It is likely that Matthew and Luke relied upon separate, perhaps oral, traditions, but differences between them do not affect the importance of the New Testament genealogies.

JOSEPH SMITH'S TEACHINGS

Luke 1:5–23. "Zacharias plead[ed] with the Lord in the temple that he might have seed, so that the priesthood might be preserved" (Discourse, 21 March 1841, recorded by William P. McIntire, The Joseph Smith Papers, accessed 21 February 2014, http://josephsmithpapers.org/paperSummary/discourse-21 -march-1841-as-reported-by-william-p-mcintire?p=1; see also Jackson, *Joseph Smith's Commentary,* 119).

"The priesthood was given to Aaron and his posterity throughout all generations. We can trace the lineage down to Zacharias, he being the only lawful administrator in his day. And the Jews knew it well, for they always acknowledged the priesthood. Zacharias, having no children, knew that the promise of God must fail. Consequently, he went into the temple to wrestle with God, according to the order of the priesthood, to obtain a promise of a son. And when the angel told him that his promise was granted, he, because of unbelief, was struck dumb" (Discourse, 23 July 1843, recorded by James Burgess, as cited in Jackson, *Joseph Smith's Commentary,* 119; see also Ehat and Cook, *Words of Joseph Smith,* 235).

STUDY QUESTIONS

1. What was John the Baptist's specific role in preparing the way of the Messiah?
2. What are the differences between the accounts of the annunciation to Zacharias and to Mary?
3. How does Luke portray Mary's role as mother?

CHAPTER 8

THE BABE OF
BETHLEHEM

Chapter 8 focuses on Jesus's birth in Bethlehem from the perspective of Matthew and Luke. Both Gospel authors share information about the events that followed during an undisclosed period of time, perhaps two years. Notice that Luke mentions Jesus as an "infant," whereas Matthew calls Him a "child," suggesting a longer period of time between His birth and the visit of the wise men and Herod's attempt to kill Him.

According to the New Testament accounts, Herod ordered the slaying of all the children in Bethlehem and the surrounding area who were two years of age and under. Herod supposed that by killing Jesus, he would be able to put an end to the Messiah (Matthew 2:6–8). With this story of hostility toward Jesus, Matthew introduces another instance where Joseph, the earthly guardian of Jesus, was guided through a divinely given dream (echoing events in the life of Joseph of Egypt). Again facing opposition to his family, Joseph was able to see a way forward and keep his family safe. Indeed, in the first two chapters of Matthew's Gospel, Joseph is the savior of Mary and Jesus. We may also detect another type: Jesus is the new Moses, who also survived a slaughter of innocent children, gave the law on a mount, and delivered his people.

Elder Talmage interrupts his discussion about events in the land of Israel to provide an account of what was happening at the same time in the Book of Mormon lands. Just as the Old Testament prophets had testified of the coming of the Messiah, so had the Nephite and Lamanite prophets "foretold in great plainness the early advent of the Lord" (100).

SINCE 1915

Candlestick. When discussing the furnishings of the ancient tabernacle and temple, the King James Version (1611) mentions the seven-branched candlestick that stood in the holy place (Exodus 25:31–40). In the seventeenth century, it made perfect sense to use the word "candlestick" because candles were the primary source of indoor light. However, oil lamps were used for lighting in the first century AD. Modern translations often substitute the word "lampstand" for "candlestick."

The taxation (Luke 2:1). To the modern reader, the word "taxed" implies a monetary assessment on personal wealth, but the taxation mentioned here was actually an enrollment, or census. In the Roman period, several such censuses were conducted in which individuals were counted by a legal administrator—and the data would then be used for the purposes of taxation and other civic business.

Modern readers should be cautious about placing the census mentioned in Luke 2 in the year of Jesus's birth. The chapter begins "And it came to pass in those days," but this merely approximates the time period and probably was not intended to refer to the year Joseph and Mary traveled to Bethlehem. Today, we understand that the census under Cyrenius ("Quirinius" in other sources) actually took place in AD 6 (KJV Luke 2:2). The Gospels are united in placing the birth year of Jesus during the tenure of Herod the Great, who died in March of 4 BC. Jesus therefore could not have been born in the same year as the census of Cyrenius.

We also know this census was a controversial action; Acts 5:37 records that a Judas of Galilee started a revolt in response to the decree.

The inn. The "inn" where Jesus was born was not a hotel where rooms were rented for the night for a modest fee. The Greek word is *kataluma,* meaning either a room attached to a personal dwelling—likely that of a family member or close friend of Joseph's or Mary's family, or a room that was a kind of communal gathering place where travelers slept for the night, sometimes referred to as a caravansary. Therefore, the story is meant not to focus on a heartless innkeeper but to explain why Jesus was born in a manger.

Herod the Great. Herod the Great was likely born in Jerusalem, where his father served the Hasmonean (Jewish) king as a chief advisor. Herod was the grandson of a convert to Judaism, and he married a Jewish princess. Because we do not have Herod's own autobiography, our information about him comes from sources that are often critical of him. Josephus, the most detailed source about Herod, drew extensively on the writings of Herod's biographer, Nicolas of Damascus.

Herod the Great quickly ascended the ranks of power and was appointed governor of Galilee at the young age of twenty-five.

Within five years of that appointment, Rome made him ruler of Judea and Galilee and gave him the title of king.

Herod undertook massive building projects and was responsible for rebuilding the temple in Jerusalem on a grand scale; consequently, it became known as Herod's temple. He built an impressive fortification at Herodium, where he was eventually buried, and he updated and strengthened the fortress at Masada. He also built the imposing seaport city of Caesarea Maritima, located on the Mediterranean.

Rome required its client-kings to maintain peace and tranquility in the provinces so trade would flourish and taxes and tolls would continue to flow into the coffers of the empire. Herod was exceptionally good at keeping the peace through despotic means.

Toward the end of Herod's life, during the time when Jesus was born in Bethlehem, Herod apparently suffered a mental breakdown and acted more violently and capriciously than he previously had. His final years were his worst, and his enemies, rivals, and the innocent suffered. His attack on the children of Bethlehem and on God's divine Son occurred during this period of Herod's life.

Matthew, providing a wider view, preserves the words of an angel who visited Joseph in Egypt: "Arise, and take the young child and his mother, and go into the land of Israel: *for they are dead which sought the young child's life*" (Matthew 2:20; emphasis added), perhaps suggesting that Herod was not alone in his opposition to the young child.

Herod Archelaus. When Herod the Great died in 4 BC, his kingdom was divided among his sons. One of them, Herod Archelaus, was awarded the region of Judea, Samaria, and Idumea. Within ten years, Archelaus was deposed and banished to Gaul (modern France), where he died sometime before AD

18. Instead of replacing him on the Jewish throne, the Romans took direct control of Judea and sent Coponius as the first Roman prefect.

The date of Jesus's birth. Early Christians apparently did not celebrate Jesus's birthday, and debates arose in later centuries when Christians began to do so. However, Matthew indicates that Jesus was born before Herod died. Because historical sources place Herod's death at 4 BC, Jesus would have been born sometime in 5 BC to 4 BC. Elder Talmage reasoned that Jesus must have been born on 6 April 1 BC, based on his interpretation of Doctrine and Covenants 20:1 (104).

Joseph Smith Translation

The Joseph Smith Translation contains several noteworthy insights into historical details of the birth narratives, particularly concerning what the Jews expected concerning the coming of the Messiah. Substantial changes are found mostly in Matthew's account of Jesus's birth. Beginning with the opening inquiry by the wise men, the JST reads, "Saying, Where is *the child* that is born *the Messiah* of the Jews?" (JST Matthew 2:2; italics indicate changes to the KJV text). The title "Messiah" seems to imply that the wise men were familiar with it from one or more Jewish sources. Although they were watching for his star in the East and recognized it when it appeared, their apparent lack of familiarity with the prophecy and traditions regarding where the Messiah would be born may suggest that they were not Jews themselves.

Study Questions

1. What did Joseph and Mary gain from the witnesses given by the shepherds and the wise men?

2. What aspects of the traditional Christmas story are found in the scriptures? What aspects of the traditional Christmas story are not found in the scriptures?

3. How do you feel when you read the story about Jesus's birth?

CHAPTER 9

THE BOY OF
NAZARETH

Elder Talmage reviews, mainly through the Gospel of Luke, the story of Jesus's boyhood, youth, and early manhood in Nazareth.

Luke's story that began with the Annunciation continues with the poignant account of Jesus's visit to Jerusalem when He was twelve years old. While His mother and Joseph began their return trip to Nazareth, the young Jesus remained in Jerusalem in the temple. Clearly, although Joseph and Mary were distraught concerning Jesus's whereabouts, Mary's son was aware of His life's mission.

Also of importance in this chapter is the discussion of how Jesus grew and learned the things of the Lord: "And Jesus increased in wisdom and stature, and in favour with God and man" (Luke 2:52). Although Jesus was the Son of God, Luke reports that He "increased" in His understanding; thus, like others of God's children, He did not come to earth with a perfect knowledge but obtained His knowledge through experience, study, and prayer. Restoration scripture provides additional insights into this period of Jesus's life (Doctrine and Covenants 93:12–14).

SINCE 1915

Nazareth. Beginning in 2009, archaeologists working in the modern, crowded city of Nazareth have made several interesting discoveries. For example, a small and modest courtyard home from the first century has been revealed for the first time. Archaeologists suggest that the village, consisting of not more than fifty homes within a very small area, had between two hundred and four hundred inhabitants, who cultivated grapes and olives.

Joseph. Mary's husband is identified in the Greek New Testament as a *tektōn,* one who worked with his hands in wood and stone, expanding our view of Joseph the carpenter.

JOSEPH SMITH'S TEACHINGS

Luke 2:51–52. "Even Jesus, the Son of God, had to refrain from [revealing all He knew], and had to restrain His feelings many times for the safety of Himself and His followers, and had to conceal the righteous purposes of His heart in relation to many things pertaining to His Father's kingdom. When still a boy He had all the intelligence necessary to enable Him to rule and govern the kingdom of the Jews, and could reason with the wisest and most profound doctors of law and divinity, and make their theories and practice to appear like folly compared with the wisdom He possessed; but He was a boy only, and lacked physical strength even to defend His own person; and was subject to cold, to hunger and to death" (27 June 1844, Manuscript History of the Church, 7:177, Church History Library, The Church of Jesus Christ of Latter-day Saints, Salt Lake City, Utah).

JOSEPH SMITH TRANSLATION

The Joseph Smith Translation inserts three sentences following the end of Matthew 2:23 in the KJV: "And he came and dwelt in a city called Nazareth: that it might be fulfilled which was spoken by the prophets, He shall be called a Nazarene. *And it came to pass, that Jesus grew up with his brethren, and waxed strong, and waited upon the Lord for the time of his ministry to come. And he served under his father, and he spake not as other men, neither could he be taught; for he needed not that any man should teach him. And after many years, the hour of his ministry drew nigh*" (JST Matthew 2:23; italics indicate changes to the KJV text).

The information contained in this extra verse moves well beyond the original context and connects the birth of Jesus to the adult ministry of the Lord, which begins in Matthew 3. This bridge verse also offers a glimpse into the spiritual and emotional development of the Lord as He prepared for His public ministry and His eventual death at Golgotha.

STUDY QUESTIONS

1. Only one event is mentioned from the boyhood of Jesus. How does Elder Talmage treat this event and its importance in the ministry of Jesus Christ?

2. What do you think it means that Mary "kept all these sayings in her heart" (Luke 2:51)?

3. How can you "increase in wisdom and stature, and in favor with God and man" (Luke 2:52)?

CHAPTER 10

IN THE WILDERNESS
OF JUDEA

Key to the beginning of Jesus's ministry were John the Baptist's testimony of Jesus and John's efforts to prepare the way for Him. We do not know how many people heard John teach or how many accepted his call to repent and be baptized, but great excitement surrounded his ministry. According to the Gospels, Pharisees and Sadducees, people who traditionally opposed one another, went to see for themselves what John was doing: "Then went out to him Jerusalem, and all Judea, and all the region round about Jordan. . . . Pharisees and Sadducees" (Matthew 3:5, 7).

Apparently, John had a great pull on the hearts of the people; the scripture describes it in broad terms: "all Judea" went to see him. As a result, "all Judea" became part of the preparation for Jesus's ministry. The interval between John's teaching and the beginning of Jesus's ministry allowed the people time to ponder John's message of repentance and prepare their hearts for Jesus

Christ's message: "The time is fulfilled, and the kingdom of God is at hand: repent ye, and believe the gospel" (Mark 1:15).

The Gospel of John the Apostle most closely follows Jesus's ministry in Judea and Jerusalem. Because he was a disciple of John the Baptist before becoming a follower of Jesus, he may have understood better than the other Gospel writers the connection between the teachings of John the Baptist and the role the Baptist played in preparing the way for the Lord in Judea and Jerusalem (see John 1:35–40, in which two disciples are mentioned. Scholars generally assume that the unnamed disciple is John, the author of the Gospel).

The highlight of this chapter in *Jesus the Christ* is the record of the baptism of Jesus, a story that has many implications for the Savior's ministry. The event raises questions that cry out for answers: Why did someone who was perfect need an ordinance that is typically associated with cleansing and the remission of sins? Why did such great spiritual manifestations take place at Jesus's baptism? Both modern revelation and the scriptural accounts help to answer these important questions.

Why was Jesus baptized? "John forbad him, saying, I have need to be baptized of thee, and comest thou to me? And Jesus answering said unto him, Suffer it to be so now: for thus it becometh us to fulfil all righteousness. Then he suffered him" (Matthew 3:14–15).

The meaning of these verses is straightforward. John the Baptist declared that if anyone needed to be baptized, it was he, John, rather than the Savior. Jesus responded by stating that John should allow Him to be baptized ("suffer it to be so now") because the ordinance would "fulfil all righteousness."

The Book of Mormon helps us understand what is meant by this phrase: "And now, if the Lamb of God, he being holy, should have need to be baptized by water, to fulfil all righteousness, O then, how much more need have we, being unholy, to be baptized, yea, even by water! And now, I would ask of you, my beloved brethren, wherein the Lamb of God did fulfil all righteousness in being baptized by water? Know ye not that he was holy? But notwithstanding he being holy, he showeth unto the children of men that, according to the flesh he humbleth himself before the Father, and witnesseth unto the Father that he would be obedient unto him in keeping his commandments" (2 Nephi 31:5–7).

In the testimony of these two witnesses (the Bible and the Book of Mormon), we learn that in being baptized, Jesus confirmed His humility and set an example to show us the way.

The baptism of Jesus was attended by great signs, including the sign of the dove's presence and the voice of the Father declaring, "Thou art my beloved Son, in whom I am well pleased" (Mark 1:11). The sign of the dove confirmed to the faithful that the Holy Ghost also testified of the importance and consequence of the events taking place and to testify to John the Baptist that he had indeed baptized the Lamb of God (John 1:32–33).

Shortly after Jesus's baptism, He journeyed into the wilderness to fast and "to be with God" (JST Matthew 4:1). Although His death was as many as three years away, the Gospel accounts of His temptations suggest that the end of His life had already come into greater focus for Him. His fast in the wilderness completed, Jesus was faced with three powerful temptations. Matthew and Luke record them in the greatest detail; Mark mentions them briefly, and John omits the story completely. In reality, we know very little about the temptations and what occurred between Jesus and the devil. The account itself is not the product of eyewitnesses; either Jesus or the Spirit revealed these events at a later time.

According to the record, Satan tried to sow doubt in Jesus's mind by asking questions beginning with "if," and Jesus strongly rebuked Satan in his efforts to tempt Him. As a prelude to Jesus's mortal ministry, this event was formative in His preparations. It offered the Savior an opportunity to probe the question of the necessity of His own death and how it fit into God's plan of salvation. During the temptations, Jesus experienced the reality of Satan, and He proved the strength of His own resolve. The plan of salvation required that He be stronger than Satan's temptations, but perhaps His resolve had not been sufficiently proven until that point.

Since 1915

John's clothing and diet. John the Baptist is one of the few people in the New Testament about whose clothing a comment is offered. What he wore was obviously different from what others wore, but there may be other reasons for the interest in John's clothing. First, it had strong similarities to the clothing worn by Elijah: "And they answered him, He was an hairy man, and girt with a girdle of leather about his loins. And he said, It is Elijah the Tishbite" (2 Kings 1:8). The Gospel authors may have wanted to draw a parallel with that Old Testament prophet.

Second, John may have taken upon himself a Nazarite vow (Numbers 6), although this is uncertain. The Nazarite vow was not precise in its obligations, and the person who took the vow determined some portion of it. Individuals may choose to avoid alcoholic drink, sexual relations, and certain foods during the duration of the vow. The individual also chose how long he or she would observe the vow. John may have *chosen* a strict diet (i.e., locusts and honey) and to live the way Elijah did.

First-century baptism. The term *baptism* in English derives from the Greek word *baptizo* and means to immerse someone or something in water. In the first century AD, baptism may have been an ordinance required of Gentiles who wished to join the Jewish faith. For individuals who were ethnic Jews, baptism was not required, but some Jews followed a practice of ritual washing by complete immersion in a *mikveh* (ritual immersion pool), rendering them clean from sin.

This practice was observed for the purpose of maintaining ritual purity; therefore, Jews immersed themselves prior to going into the temple or after having become impure through contact with something unclean, such as a dead body. The mikveh ritual was observed many times each year, whereas the Christian practice of baptism was a single event to signify conversion to the faith and departure from a life of sin. The baptism performed by John the Baptist was thus an ordinance that signified a new dispensation heralded by a new prophet—a new legal administrator.

Publicans. The term *publicans* refers to anyone employed by Rome or her client-kings and leaders to supply or outfit the Roman army in the region or to those who may have been employed collecting taxes, tolls, or rents. Jews who served in these capacities often faced ostracism in their communities and might be cast out of the synagogues, which was a form of excommunication. The publicans had no distinct religious beliefs or practices but were marginalized for accepting employment from Roman sources. Like other members of the royal bureaucracy during this period, some publicans may have fulfilled their duties faithfully and fairly, and others may have taken advantage of their position over the common people.

Joseph Smith's Teachings

Mark 1:4. "John came preaching the gospel for the remission of sins. He had his authority from God, and the oracles of God were with him. The kingdom of [God] for a season seemed to be with John alone. . . . He preached the same gospel and baptism that Jesus and the apostles preached after him" (Discourse, 22 January 1843, recorded by Wilford Woodruff, as cited in Jackson, *Joseph Smith's Commentary*, 116).

Matthew 3:16. "The dove which sat upon his shoulder was a sure testimony that he was of God" (Discourse, [21 March] 1841, reported by Martha Jane Knowlton Coray, The Joseph Smith Papers, accessed 21 February 2014, http://josephsmithpapers .org/paperSummary/discourse-21-march-1841-as-reported-by -martha-jane-knowlton-coray?p=3; see also Jackson, *Joseph Smith's Commentary*, 79).

"[The sign of the dove was] instituted before the creation. [The] Devil could not come in [the] sign of a dove. [The] Holy Ghost is a personage in the form of a personage. [He] does not confine [himself] to [the] form of a dove, but in [the] sign of a dove" (Discourse, 29 January 1843, recorded by Willard Richards, as cited in Jackson, *Joseph Smith's Commentary*, 79; see also The Joseph Smith Papers, accessed 21 February 2014, http:// josephsmithpapers.org/paperSummary/journal-december-1842 -june-1844-book-1-21-december-1842-10-march-1843?p=163).

Joseph Smith Translation

If this section of the Joseph Smith Translation could be characterized simply, the result would be that it emphasizes witnessing, or bearing witness. Specifically, the changes to the New Testament in these chapters of Matthew and John bring to the forefront the testimony of John the Baptist.

Matthew 3:8 is almost entirely new: "*Why is it, that ye receive not the preaching of him whom God hath sent? If ye receive not this in your hearts, ye receive not me; and if ye receive not me, ye receive not him of whom I am sent to bear record; and for your sins ye have no cloak. Repent therefore, and* bring forth fruits meet for repentance" (JST Matthew 3:8; italics indicate changes to the KJV text).

A second addition to the Gospel of Matthew offers a more panoramic view of John's witness of Jesus: "*And it is he of whom I shall bear record,* whose fan *shall be* in his hand, and he will thoroughly purge his floor, and gather his wheat into the garner; but *in the fullness of his own time* will burn up the chaff with un-quenchable fire. *Thus came John, preaching and baptizing in the river of Jordan; bearing record, that he who was coming after him, had power to baptize with the Holy Ghost and fire*" (JST Matthew 3:12; italics indicate changes to the KJV text).

The Prophet Joseph Smith's own experience led him to emend John 1:18. The KJV statement declares that "no man hath seen God at any time," which was untrue regarding both the Old Testament and Joseph's experience in the Sacred Grove. He revised the verse to read, "*And* no man hath seen God at any time, *except he hath borne record of the Son; for except it is through him no man can be saved*" (JST John 1:18; italics indicate changes to the KJV text). The doctrinal clarification here is important because of all the times in Bible history when prophets conversed with the Lord as He led them and taught them His truths. Indeed, every one of the standard works relates personal visits with the Lord. Without Joseph Smith's additions, John 1:18 contradicts every other book of scripture.

STUDY QUESTIONS

1. What is the importance of John the Baptist and his mission?
2. In what ways are modern prophets and apostles preparing the world for the Second Coming of the Messiah?
3. How can you make the sacrament a more powerful symbol of your renewal of the commitments you made at your baptism?

CHAPTER 11

FROM JUDEA
TO GALILEE

Toward the beginning of chapter 11, Elder Talmage states, "John's testimony, that Jesus was the Redeemer of the world, was declared as boldly as had been his message of the imminent coming of the Lord. 'Behold the Lamb of God, which taketh away the sin of the world,' he proclaimed; and, that none might fail to comprehend his identification of the Christ, he added: 'This is he of whom I said, After me cometh a man which is preferred before me: for he was before me'" (139).

Identifying Jesus as the "Lamb" or "Lamb of God" is one of John's favorite symbols for the Savior, both in his Gospel and in the book of Revelation, where he calls the Lord "the Lamb slain from the foundation of the world" (Revelation 13:8). After John the Baptist testified that Jesus was indeed the Lamb of God, at least two of his followers began to follow Jesus (John 1:35–40).

Soon after John's declaration concerning Him, Jesus attended a wedding in Cana of Galilee. When the wine was gone, Jesus performed His first recorded miracle by changing water to wine. As Elder Talmage carefully notes, Jesus's mother held a special position of authority on the occasion, suggesting that the wedding may have been that of a close family member, perhaps even one of Jesus's siblings (144).

The four Gospel accounts show some diversity in the order of events after Jesus's baptism and wilderness fast. All the Gospel writers agree that at least some of the Apostles were chosen prior to the Sermon on the Mount and that some early miracles drew people to the Savior. Elder Talmage focuses mainly on the Gospel of John; then, in subsequent chapters (chapter 16 and following), he returns to the order of events in the Gospel of Matthew. The order in which these early events occurred is not important from a doctrinal perspective, although the resulting questions are of great historical interest. Of more significance is how early events such as John's testimony of Jesus as the Lamb of God and the miracle of turning water into wine shaped the followers of Jesus and how these events prepared Jesus to atone for the sins of humankind.

Since 1915

Galilee. In the synoptic Gospels, most of Jesus's ministry takes place in Galilee or, more properly, *the* Galilee. *Galilee* means "circle" and included the region encircling the Sea of Galilee, a freshwater lake. Jesus and His disciples most frequently visited the region on the north shore of the Sea of Galilee and included important villages and towns such as Capernaum, Chorazin, Bethsaida, and others. With the exception of Judas Iscariot, all of Jesus's original twelve Apostles were Galileans. Recent archaeological discoveries, including the 1986 discovery of a first-century fishing boat, show that Galilee was a Jewish region with an economy based mostly on agrarian pursuits (wheat, olives, and viticulture), fishing, pottery, and millstone production.

Tiberias and Sepphoris were the two largest cities in Galilee, and both had a veneer typical of other Greco-Roman cities in the region. Recent archaeological work at both sites continues to provide additional insight into the social, religious, political, and economic setting of Jesus's ministry. Interestingly, the Gospels do not mention any visits by Jesus to these cities.

Old and New Testament names. The Old Testament was written in Hebrew, with a few sections in Aramaic. The New Testament was written in Greek; in Greek, endings of Hebrew names were changed to an "s": Judah became Judas; Messiah became Messias; Zechariah became Zacharias; Isaiah became Esaias; Jeremiah became Jeremias; and Elijah became Elias.

Through the revelations of the Restoration, we learn that *Elias* may be used to denote a person or a calling to be a forerunner. Elijah was an Old Testament prophet who held the sealing power. Most instances of the word *Elias* in the King James Version of the Bible are a Greek translation of the name *Elijah*.

Joseph Smith's Teachings

John 1:36. Echoing John the Baptist's language, Joseph Smith taught, "God clearly manifested . . . the redemption which he prepared by offering the Messiah as a Lamb slain from before the foundation of the world" ("To the Elders of the Church of Latter Day Saints," *Messenger and Advocate,* November 1835, 209).

Joseph Smith Translation

A significant change occurs in Luke 3 in the Joseph Smith Translation, where a complete paragraph has been added. The change to this verse characterizes many of the other changes in the JST and offers an overview of what the prophets foretold regarding Jesus's ministry. The key part of the addition reads: "Prepare ye the way of the Lord, *and* make his paths straight. *For behold, and lo, he shall come as it is written in the book of the prophets, to take away the sins of the world, and to bring salvation unto the heathen nations; to gather together those who are lost, which are of the sheepfold of Israel; yea, even her dispersed and afflicted; and also to prepare the way, and make possible the preaching of the gospel unto the Gentiles*" (JST Luke 3:4; italics indicate changes to the KJV text).

A related change in John 3 connects the teachings of the prophets from the Old Testament with the manner in which they foretold of Jesus's ministry: "He *who* believeth on him is not condemned: but he *who* believeth not is condemned already, because he hath not believed *on* the name of the only begotten Son of God, *which before was preached by the mouth of the holy prophets; for they testified of me*" (JST John 3:18; italics indicate changes to the KJV text).

STUDY QUESTIONS

1. How does the miracle at Cana set the tone for Jesus's ministry?
2. Why does Elder Talmage discuss the nature of miracles? How does Elder Talmage's discussion help you understand miracles?
3. How did you feel the last time you witnessed a miracle in your life?

CHAPTER 12

EARLY INCIDENTS IN OUR LORD'S PUBLIC MINISTRY

The synoptic Gospels place the cleansing of the temple at the end of Jesus's public ministry on the day of the triumphal entry into Jerusalem (Matthew 21:12–16), whereas the Gospel of John places the event at the beginning of the ministry immediately after the wedding at Cana (John 2:13–17). Because the two events are described with similar details, some scholars have wondered whether John moved the cleansing of the temple to the beginning of the story to explain why the Jewish leaders in Jerusalem felt so much hatred toward Jesus.

In either case, whether two distinct events or just one took place, the cleansing of the temple was a provocative act that would have offended Jewish religious sensibilities and caused many to call for Jesus to be punished. If someone other than Jesus had acted to cleanse the temple, even the modern reader would expect the offender to be punished according to the law. Although many Jews did not feel that was the case, the Essenes, for example, had distanced themselves from the temple, waiting for a time when it would be purified.

Two events stand out from the early period of Jesus's ministry that define His teaching style and the way others came to believe in Him. Nicodemus, a Pharisee from Judea, approached Jesus with a question. In the ensuing interchange, Nicodemus pursued a line of reasoning that was starkly literal, even if it meant asking nonsensical questions. In some ways, Nicodemus was a personification of the literalism associated with first-century Jewish legalism. Jesus responded with words that favored the spiritual side of belief, stating, "If I have told you earthly things, and ye believe not, how shall ye believe, if I tell you of heavenly things? And no man hath ascended up to heaven, but he that came down from heaven, even the Son of man which is in heaven" (John 3:12–13).

In this interchange, we see the contrasts in types of belief— the heavenly and the earthly—that characterize the Gospel of John. Jesus was sent from above to testify of the truths His Father had given Him. For Nicodemus, who came to Jesus in the night (an important symbol to John of opposition and spiritual darkness), these truths were beyond his comprehension. One of the highlights of this exchange is that Jesus offered the clearest statement of His ministry as a consequence of the discussion about literalism: "For God so loved the world, that he gave his only begotten Son, that whosoever believeth in him should not perish, but have everlasting life" (John 3:16). No greater testimony personally expressed by Jesus is found in the Gospels, and it came as a response to someone who did not yet comprehend the light of the gospel. Thus, the journey of Nicodemus represents the journey of believers from darkness into light, where they can comprehend the full scope of Jesus's mission.

SINCE 1915

The functions of the Jerusalem temple. Before its destruction by the Romans in August AD 70, the Jerusalem temple was the center place of religious worship in the first century. Only a small section of the first-century temple retaining wall remains, a section of which is known as the Western Wall (or *Kotel*).

The ancient temple functioned differently in many respects from a modern Latter-day Saint temple; its primary purposes were for the sacrifice of animals associated with the requirements of the law of Moses, as well as for prayer services (Luke 1:8–10; cf. Acts 3:1). The heart and soul of the temple were its altars, including the enormous altar where animal sacrifices were performed and the much smaller altar in the Holy Place where the daily incense was burned just outside the Holy of Holies. The Holy of Holies was an empty room in Jesus's day, but at one time it housed the ark of the covenant. Many scholars now believe the area once covered by the Holy of Holies is encompassed by the Dome of the Rock, an early Islamic structure.

Only priests and Levites were permitted to ascend the altar of sacrifice or enter into the temple building where the altar of incense stood. All other Israelites were required to observe sacrifices from a distance. Large outer courts were built around the temple, but entrance into the temple itself was forbidden to everyone but the priests.

JOSEPH SMITH'S TEACHINGS

Mark 2:15–17. "Christ said he came to call sinners to repentance and save them. Christ was condemned by the righteous Jews because he took sinners into his society. He took them upon the principle that they repented of their sins" (Discourse, 9 June 1842, recorded by Eliza R. Snow, The Joseph Smith

Papers, accessed 21 February 2014, http://josephsmithpapers.org
/paperSummary/nauvoo-relief-society-minute-book?p=58; see
also Jackson, *Joseph Smith's Commentary,* 117).

JOSEPH SMITH TRANSLATION

Jesus's cleansing of the temple prefigured these words from
later in His ministry: "*And he said unto them, Behold ye these stones
of the temple, and all this great work, and buildings of the temple?
Verily I say unto you, they shall be thrown down and left unto the
Jews desolate.* And Jesus said unto *them, See you not all* these *things
and do you not understand them? Verily I say unto you,* there shall
not be left *here upon this temple* one stone upon another, that shall
not be thrown down" (JST Mark 13:2; italics indicate changes to
the KJV text).

STUDY QUESTIONS

1. What did Jesus accomplish by clearing the temple at the be-
    ginning of His mission? What things does the Lord want you
    to clean out of your spiritual house?
2. John 3:1–21 recounts a conversation between Jesus and
    Nicodemus, who approached the Savior by night. What do
    Jesus's words tell you about the sincerity of Nicodemus?
3. Why do you think Jesus turned His attention to the small
    villages and towns in Galilee to preach the gospel rather than
    remain in Jerusalem?

CHAPTER 13

HONORED BY STRANGERS,
REJECTED BY HIS OWN

Experiences early in the Savior's ministry, as discussed in this chapter, demonstrate the differing responses people had to Jesus and His teachings. In one case, for example, a woman withstood rebuke, came to faith, and opened a door for the proselytizing of her people (172–77). In another instance, some were offended when Jesus offered an interpretation of scripture that openly declared Him as the long-awaited Messiah (179–81).

Unlike Nicodemus, the Samaritan woman met Jesus at midday. Because John appreciated the contrast between light and darkness, he may have intended that we see a contrast between Nicodemus and the Samaritan woman at the well in their understanding of Jesus's message. That is, Nicodemus sought him at night and initially did not understand, but the Samaritan woman, who saw Him at midday, was enlightened by Jesus's words.

In this atypical exchange—women and men unrelated to each other did not typically converse in public, nor did Jews communicate with Samaritans—the woman asked Jesus several pointed questions. First, she asked Him, "How is it that thou, being a Jew, askest drink of me, which am a woman of Samaria? for the Jews have no dealings with the Samaritans" (John 4:9). Jesus responded with equally pointed language, "Ye worship ye know not what: we know what we worship: for salvation is of the Jews" (John 4:22).

The woman's path to faith was precipitated by a mild rebuke from Jesus, the omniscient Teacher. "Go," He said, "call thy husband, and come hither" (John 4:16). Jesus knew her response before she gave it: "I have no husband." He seized the moment and said, "Thou hast well said, I have no husband: For thou hast had five husbands; and he whom thou now hast is not thy husband: in that saidst thou truly" (John 4:17–18). In that rebuke, the woman began to realize that Jesus was a prophet, an incomplete understanding, but she had already come a long way in her understanding in a short space of time. By the time their conversation ended, the woman had declared that Jesus was the Messiah she and her people had anticipated (John 4:25–26).

Following His encounter with the Samaritan woman, Jesus traveled to Nazareth. In the synagogue there, He read to the congregation a passage from Isaiah 61:1–3: "And he closed the book, and he gave it again to the minister, and sat down. And the eyes of all them that were in the synagogue were fastened on him. And he began to say unto them, This day is this scripture fulfilled in your ears. And all bare him witness, and wondered at the gracious words which proceeded out of his mouth. And they said, Is not this Joseph's son?" (Luke 4:20–22).

The passage in question from Isaiah was understood to be a prophecy of the coming of the Messiah and His ministry to the poor and downtrodden. When Jesus testified that those words had been "fulfilled in your ears," it was tantamount to declaring that Jesus *was* the promised Messiah. After reading about the newfound faith of the Samaritan woman, we might expect to learn that when Jesus openly declared His mission in his hometown, His hearers accepted Him. Instead, many of those in the Nazareth synagogue rejected Jesus's testimony and sought to kill Him (Luke 4:28–30). Unfortunately, this was only one of several occasions with such an outcome.

Contrasting the Samaritan woman with the people of Nazareth proves a powerful reality: faith is something that is not easily bestowed because it requires something from the listener.

The chapter ends when Jesus travels to Capernaum, where people were amazed at what they heard and saw (Mark 1:21–28).

Since 1915

Samaritans. The Samaritans were related ethnically to Jews living in Judea and Galilee at the time of Jesus, but their ancestors more than six centuries before the opening of the New Testament had intermingled with foreigners brought to the area by the kings of Assyria and Babylon and thus were no longer ethnically pure. Because of racial intermixing and other offenses, the Samaritans were despised by the Jews of Judea and Galilee. The Jews were in turn despised by the Samaritans.

When the Samaritans were forbidden to worship in Jerusalem during the intertestamental period, they built an alternative temple on Mt. Gerizim, some forty miles north of Jerusalem. A Hasmonean (Jewish) army later destroyed this Samaritan temple, further inflaming the animosity between the two groups. The Samaritans accepted the Torah as scripture, but their version differed from the Hebrew Torah, which widened the religious gap between the two groups.

In part because of the faith of the woman at the well in Samaria, the Apostles taught the gospel there shortly after Jesus's death (Acts 8:5–9). By permitting Samaritans to attend their worship services, early Jewish Christians may have offended other Jews who viewed the Samaritans as an impure people.

"God is a Spirit." This phrase from John 4:24, "God is a Spirit," causes concern for modern readers because it appears to endorse an incorporeal deity. The belief that God has a body is central to Latter-day Saint beliefs. The printed King James Version places the verb "is" in italics because the word "is" is not directly evident from the Greek; it is also important to note that the "a" is also not clearly indicated in the Greek. John may just as well have meant "God is Spirit" or even "God is spiritual." The Joseph Smith Translation, however, clarifies the meaning of the passage: "*For unto such hath* God *promised his* Spirit" (JST John 4:24; italics indicate changes in the KJV text).

The context of this verse helps determine what John intended. Jesus was teaching the woman of Samaria about true worship of God: "But the hour cometh, and now is, when the true worshippers shall worship the Father in spirit and in truth: for the Father seeketh such to worship him" (John 4:23). The intent seems to have been to teach the woman that Jewish exclusivism would soon end and that everyone who wished to worship God would do so through the Spirit. The words "God is a Spirit" follow immediately in the next verse, and if we accept them as they appear in the KJV, perhaps the Lord was communicating the idea that we approach God through spiritual means, not that God is made only of spirit matter. The JST translation of the verse offers a similar understanding of the verse: "For unto such hath God promised his Spirit; *and they who worship him, must worship in spirit and in truth*" (JST John 4:24; emphasis added).

Joseph Smith's Teachings

Genesis 1:26–28. "That which is without body or parts is nothing. There is no other God in heaven but that God who has flesh and bones" (Discourse, 5 January 1841, reported by William Clayton, The Joseph Smith Papers, accessed 21 February 2014, http://josephsmithpapers.org/paperSummary/discourse-5-january-1841-as-reported-by-william-clayton?p=4; see also Jackson, *Joseph Smith's Commentary*, 6).

Joseph Smith Translation

In John 4:2, the King James Version reports that Jesus did not baptize anyone, even though John 3:22 states explicitly that He did indeed baptize some of His followers: "After these things came Jesus and his disciples into the land of Judea; and there he tarried with them, and baptized." Because of the way Greek verbs are constructed, the original Greek of this verse unambiguously refers to Jesus baptizing.

The Joseph Smith Translation clarifies the problematic verse. JST John 4:1–3 reads: "When therefore the Pharisees had heard that Jesus made and baptized more disciples than John, *they sought more diligently some means that they might put him to death; for many received John as a prophet, but they believed not on Jesus. Now the Lord knew this,* though *he* himself baptized not *so many as* his disciples" (italics indicate changes to the KJV text). Thus, the JST corrects the statement in KJV John 4:2 that Jesus did not baptize.

Study Questions

1. How was the Samaritan woman influential in helping to open the door for teaching the gospel in Samaria?

2. Why do you think the people in Nazareth reacted to Jesus the way they did when He read in the synagogue?

3. Review the incident related in Mark 1:21–28. Why do you think Jesus's visit to Capernaum was so important? Identify a gospel principle that has "amazed" you and answer the following question: "Why and how does that impact me?"

CHAPTER 14

CONTINUATION OF OUR LORD'S MINISTRY IN GALILEE

Jesus was well known as a healer, and in this chapter, Elder Talmage highlights another miraculous healing, the man with leprosy who knelt before Jesus to ask for His help (188–89). A Western reader may miss the implication of Jesus's interaction with ritually impure individuals—those with leprosy, issues of blood, and the dead. In most cases, Jesus physically touched these people, breaking down barriers that had existed because of laws concerning ritual purity.

This tender story is followed by another miracle of healing. This time a man was afflicted with paralysis (190–93), and he was healed both physically and spiritually as Jesus forgave him of his sins.

Jesus continued His mission to the least, the last, and the lost when He reached out to both "publicans and sinners" (Mark 2:13–17). The chapter in *Jesus the Christ* ends when Jesus invites

Simon Peter and Andrew: "Come ye after me, and I will make you to become fishers of men" (Mark 1:17).

SINCE 1915

Modern explanation of miracles. Jesus's ministry was punctuated with miracles, as were the early acts of the Apostles in the New Testament. In the early twentieth century, biblical scholars commonly analyzed these miracles, attempting to explain them by unknown and unseen natural laws. Rather than focusing on physical explanations for miracles, however, we would profit more spiritually by understanding *why* Jesus performed miracles and the *effect* these miracles had in the lives of those blessed by them.

Symbolism in the miracles. We may identify several categories of miracles performed by Jesus Christ: (1) healings requested by individuals who were afflicted, (2) healings performed even without a request, (3) sight restored, (4) people fed, (5) deceased persons brought back to life, (6) miracles in which an individual was blessed, (7) miracles of cleansing, and (8) appearances by the resurrected Christ.

Symbolic meaning can be discerned in many of the miracles that Jesus performed, such as that of turning water to wine or the multiplying of the loaves and fishes. Noting spiritual parallels to physical events can add a deeper dimension to a personal testimony. But care should be taken not to look "beyond the mark" (Jacob 4:14).

JOSEPH SMITH'S TEACHINGS

Luke 15:11–32. "[The] dealing of God with individual men [is] always righteous. [They] always have access to [the] throne of God. . . . Servants of God of the last days, myself and those I have ordained, have the priesthood and a mission—to the publicans and sinners" (Discourse, 29 January 1843, recorded by Willard Richards, as cited in Jackson, *Joseph Smith's Commentary,* 124; see also Journal, December 1842–June 1844; Book 1, 21 December 1842–10 March 1843, The Joseph Smith Papers, accessed 21 February 2014, http://josephsmithpapers.org/paperSummary /journal-december-1842-june-1844-book-1-21-december-1842 -10-march-1843?p=168).

STUDY QUESTIONS

1. When Jesus called His Twelve Apostles, He asked them to leave everything behind, including their employment. How can you tell whether this request was an easy or a difficult decision?

2. In what ways did the publicans and sinners react to Jesus differently than they did to other people?

3. How does Jesus's discussion about the "old and new" (Mark 2:21; John 2:1–10) relate to the Restoration?

4. How can you become one of the "fishers" (Mark 1:17) of individuals where you live?

CHAPTER 15

LORD OF
THE SABBATH

In this chapter, Elder Talmage treats the subject of healing on the Sabbath and the discourse in John 5 in which Jesus testifies that He did only His Father's will.

For the modern reader, the issue of healing on the Sabbath may be puzzling—perhaps because of our modern pragmatism that favors the result rather than the method by which the result is achieved. In each of the Sabbath controversies, some observers interpret Jesus's actions as contrary to proper Sabbath observance because the action required someone to work, including God. This was a serious accusation. If Jesus's actions constituted work, whether good or evil, to any degree, then the healing could not be accepted as coming from God.

For someone unaccustomed to witnessing physical healing miracles, an encounter with the divine may raise conflicting emotions—a desire to believe the miracle is of God and an opposing thought that dismisses it as something else. Jesus's audience experienced this dilemma, and many chose not to attribute the miracles to God. "But when the Pharisees heard it, they said, This fellow doth not cast out devils, but by Beelzebub the prince of the devils" (Matthew 12:24).

As with the unbelieving people of Nazareth, even the most obvious and profound testimonies can result in hostility. Not all of the Jews were so hard-hearted, however. We should remember that many Jews accepted Jesus—His followers were Jewish, as were the original Apostles. The Jews were a people trying to understand the hand of God in their lives, each reacting differently to Jesus's ministry. The gospel was not preached to the Gentiles until after Jesus's death and Resurrection.

Since 1915

Names for the Sea of Galilee. The Sea of Galilee is an inland freshwater lake located in central Galilee. It is seven hundred feet below sea level, making it the lowest freshwater lake in the world (only the Dead Sea, a saltwater lake, is lower). The Sea of Galilee bears various names in the New Testament: the Sea of Tiberias, the lake of Kinneret, and the lake of Gennesaret. Fed by freshwater springs and the Jordan River, the Sea of Galilee is central to many of the stories of Jesus's ministry in Matthew, Mark, and Luke.

Joseph Smith Translation

At the end of the exchange between Jesus and the Pharisees regarding healing on the Sabbath, Jesus spoke of the unpardonable sin. The Joseph Smith Translation changes to these verses in Matthew 12 suggest that some in Jesus's audience were alarmed by the thought that there was an unpardonable sin, and they asked for clarification. Furthermore, the changes suggest that some sincerely wanted to understand the meaning of what Jesus taught: "*Then*

came some of the scribes and said unto him, Master, it is written, that,
Every sin shall be forgiven; but ye say, Whosoever speaketh against the
Holy Ghost shall not be forgiven. And they asked him, saying, How
can these things be? And he said unto them, When the unclean spirit
is gone out of a man, he walketh through dry places, seeking rest,
and findeth none; *but when a man speaketh against the Holy Ghost,*
Then he saith, I will return into my house from whence I came out;
and when he is come, he findeth *him* empty, swept, and garnished;
for the good spirit leaveth him unto himself" (Matthew 12:43; italics
indicate changes to the KJV text).

The changes to the wording of two verses in John are small,
but the changes in meaning are dramatic. In the original, Jesus
said, "If I bear witness of myself, my witness is *not* true" (emphasis added). Here, the JST alters the meaning by turning Jesus's
words into a positive assertion, and the following verse affirms
that there is another witness given of the truth: "*Therefore* if I
bear witness of myself, *yet* my witness is true. *For I am not alone,*
there is another *who* beareth witness of me; and I know that the
testimony which he *giveth* of me is true" (John 5:31–32; italics
indicate changes to the KJV text).

Study Questions

1. The reaction of Jesus's opponents to His healing on the
   Sabbath demonstrates their concern for keeping that day holy.
   What did Jesus teach concerning the sanctity of the Sabbath?

2. How do you feel when you have participated in true worship on the Sabbath? What can you do to improve your own
   Sabbath day observance?

3. John 5 is considered a declaration on the law of witnesses.
   What witnesses from the Gospel of John are discussed in this
   chapter?

CHAPTER 16

THE CHOSEN TWELVE

In this chapter, Elder Talmage discusses in detail the names and known histories of the various members of the original Twelve Apostles and differentiates those who share the same name. The calling of the Twelve is also discussed, as well as some of the difficulties they faced when they were asked to leave their employment and follow Christ.

Elder Talmage also provides observations about the group and distinguishes between two terms found in the New Testament: *disciple* and *apostle.* The word *disciple* denotes a student and may refer to any follower of Jesus or to one of the Twelve, perhaps because they all were His student-followers. The word *apostle* refers to someone who is "sent out" and also has both a specific meaning as a member of the Twelve and a general meaning as anyone who is sent out as a missionary to bear witness of Christ and teach about Him.

The first use of the term *apostle* is found in Luke 6:13, where

Jesus chose from His disciples twelve, "whom also he named apostles," or *apostoloi,* or in English, "ones sent out" to preach the name of Jesus. The general and specific usage of the term in the New Testament can be confusing, which led to disputes in the first-century church. As a general rule, the term is used in a specific sense (Apostle) in the Gospels and in a general sense (missionary) in Paul's letters.

SINCE 1915

James. A number of individuals in the New Testament bear the name of James, which is the English form of the Hebrew name Jacob (pronounced *Yakov*). Because Latin transliterates the name as *Iacomus* (Jacomus), the shortened form becomes *James.*

In the New Testament, several men are named *Jacob,* all translated as *James* in the King James Version: (1) the son of Zebedee (brother to John), one of Jesus's original Twelve Apostles (Matthew 10:2); (2) the son of Alphaeus, another of the Twelve (Matthew 10:3); and (3) Jesus's brother (Matthew 13:55; Mark 6:3), who is considered the author of the Epistle of James.

James and John, sons of Zebedee. The New Testament mentions James and John, the sons of Zebedee, as disciples of Jesus. They are two of the inner circle of three (Peter, James, and John) who were alone with Jesus on several important occasions. James and John initially were fishermen on the Sea of Galilee, working with their father, Zebedee. Some scholars suggest their mother was Salome, the sister of Jesus's mother, making James and John first cousins of Jesus (521; Elder Talmage provides details of this reconstruction without taking a definitive position).

Joseph Smith's Teachings

Matthew 10:1. "The apostles in ancient times held the keys of this priesthood—of the mysteries of the kingdom of God—and consequently were enabled to unlock and unravel all things pertaining to the government of the Church, the welfare of society, the future destiny of men, and the agency, power, and influence of spirits" ("Try the Spirits," *Times and Seasons,* 1 April 1842, 745, as cited in Jackson, *Joseph Smith's Commentary,* 86).

Joseph Smith Translation

One Joseph Smith Translation change to a verse in the Gospel of Luke expands the definition of discipleship in an interesting way. The change reflects the idea that anyone who *fears* to sacrifice his or her life cannot be considered a disciple of the Lord: "If any *one* come to me, and hate not his father, and mother, and wife, and children, and brethren, and sisters *or husband,* yea, and *their* own life also, *or in other words, is afraid to lay down their life for my sake,* cannot be my disciple" (JST Luke 14:26; italics indicate changes to the KJV text).

Study Questions

1. Jesus called his first Apostles on a mission shortly after calling them to follow Him. What are the similarities between their mission and a modern Latter-day Saint mission?
2. What are the general attributes and characteristics that bond the Twelve together? What are the general attributes and characteristics that bind modern prophets and apostles together?
3. What are the differences between Elder Talmage's use of *disciple* and *apostle?*

CHAPTER 17

THE SERMON ON THE MOUNT

This chapter begins with what may be the most important discourse of Jesus's ministry—the Sermon on the Mount. It is reported in two different accounts in the New Testament (Matthew 5–7; Luke 6:17–49) and in a slightly different version in the Book of Mormon (3 Nephi 12–14).

The Sermon on the Mount introduces Jesus's ministry as He began His long and winding course toward Gethsemane and Golgotha. The brilliance of the Sermon on the Mount lies in its simplicity and ability to communicate answers to real human questions.

The sermon begins with the Beatitudes that promise immediate and eternal blessings for certain behaviors. The words lay a foundation for His followers to shift their allegiance from the law of Moses to the words of Jesus.

The body of the sermon deals with timely topics, illustrating how Jesus's followers can live a principle-based existence after learning to be obedient to gospel laws, to be privately religious in a religion that requires public acts of devotion, and to judge righteously.

The core of the sermon might be considered the revelation of the higher law, or the law that would replace the law of Moses. In five instances, Jesus teaches, "Ye have heard that it was said by them of old time" (Matthew 5:21, 27, 33, 38, and 43). Each reference places a new teaching of Jesus in juxtaposition to a teaching or principle of the law of Moses or one of the traditions of the fathers, effectively providing His followers with a new law.

To clarify matters, Jesus also taught, "Think not that I am come to destroy the law, or the prophets: I am not come to destroy, but to fulfill" (Matthew 5:17). That statement does not mean He came to end the law of Moses; the Greek word meaning "to fulfill" more accurately means to complete, fill out, or accomplish. In other words, Jesus fulfilled, or accomplished, the law of Moses by giving His life as a sacrifice—which the animal sacrifices of the law of Moses had foreshadowed. This sense of continuity was likely important for first-century audiences who had lived their entire lives in obedience to the law of Moses. They were now being asked to leave behind their older law and part of their ethnic identity and follow the teachings of a living witness—the concept that the earlier law had been fulfilled would ease the transition between Judaism and Jesus's teachings.

The Restoration makes explicit what is implicit in the Bible. As Jehovah, Jesus had given Israel the original law on Mount Sinai and, as the new Moses, He now called Israel to a higher righteousness from the mount overlooking the Sea of Galilee (3 Nephi 15).

One of the key principles from the Sermon on the Mount

is Jesus's denunciation of public displays of false piety. Jesus specifically denounces those who outwardly appear to be religious but who are inwardly sinful. He compared them to actors in a Greek play, called hypocrites, who wore masks in their public performances. "Therefore," He taught, "when thou doest thine alms, do not sound a trumpet before thee, as the hypocrites do in the synagogues and in the streets, that they may have glory of men. Verily I say unto you, They have their reward" (Matthew 6:2). He also rebuked those who publicly advertised their fasting, as well as those who gave to the poor and drew attention to their actions. In this invitation to true discipleship, the Sermon on the Mount calls on all of Jesus's followers to avoid hypocrisy in their religious acts.

Since 1915

The Sermon on the Mount in the Joseph Smith Translation and Book of Mormon. Many changes made to the Bible by the Prophet Joseph Smith are included in the footnotes and the appendix of the LDS edition of the Bible. Much of the JST is contained in one of these two places, but hundreds more minor changes are not included. If the entire Joseph Smith Translation is compared to all of the changes made to Matthew 5–7, it becomes apparent that the JST and the Book of Mormon version (3 Nephi 12–14) are nearly identical. Only a few minor differences are found, such as the omission of Nephite monetary terms in the JST and the omission of such terms as "Pharisees" in the Nephite version.

Joseph Smith's Teachings

Matthew 7:21–23. Joseph Smith talked about the importance of some of the teachings in the Sermon on the Mount when he taught, "That which the world calls righteousness I have not any regard for. To be righteous is to be just and merciful. If a man fails in kindness, justice, and mercy, he will be damned" (Discourse, 21 May 1843, recorded by Martha Jane Coray, as cited in Jackson, *Joseph Smith's Commentary,* 83; see also Ehat and Cook, *Words of Joseph Smith,* 206).

JOSEPH SMITH TRANSLATION

In Matthew 5:28, Jesus teaches the higher law regarding adultery: "But I say unto you, That whosoever looketh on a woman to lust after her hath committed adultery with her already in his heart. " The Joseph Smith Translation includes an additional verse: "*Behold, I give unto you a commandment, that ye suffer none of these things to enter into your heart, for it is better that ye should deny yourselves of these things, wherein ye will take up your cross, than that ye should be cast into hell*" (JST Matthew 5:28; italics indicate changes to the KJV text). With the words "I give unto you a commandment," the JST adds power to Jesus's admonition.

During His mortal ministry, Jesus rarely used the word *commandment* to describe His teachings. On the night of the Last Supper, however, in one of His best-known statements, He said, "A new commandment I give unto you, That ye love one another; as I have loved you, that ye also love one another" (John 13:34).

Three additions to the final chapter of the Sermon on the Mount clarify what and why the disciples should teach. The first addition contains a directive to the disciples to rebuke the Jewish leaders for their hypocrisy: "*And Jesus said unto his disciples, beholdest thou the Scribes, and the Pharisees, and the Priests, and the Levites? They teach in their synagogues but do not observe the law, nor the commandments; and all have gone out of the way, and are under sin. Go thou and say unto them, Why teach ye men the law and the commandments, when ye yourselves are the children of corruption?"* (JST Matthew 7:4; italics indicate changes to the KJV text).

The second addition instructs the Apostles: *"Go ye into the world, saying unto all, Repent, for the kingdom of heaven has come nigh unto you. And the mysteries of the kingdom ye shall keep within yourselves; for it is not meet to* give that which is holy unto the dogs" (JST Matthew 7:6; italics indicate changes to the KJV text).

The third addition to Matthew 7 begins with the Apostles expressing concern that their testimony will be rejected and that the Jews will not believe there can be any new word from God: *"And then said his disciples unto him, They will say unto us, We ourselves are righteous and need not that any man should teach us; God, we know, heard Moses, and some of the prophets; but us he will not hear. And they will say, We have the law for our salvation, and that is sufficient for us"* (JST Matthew 7:9; italics indicate changes to the KJV text).

Jesus's reply assures His Apostles and those they teach that God stands ever ready to bless those who come to Him: *"Jesus answered, and said unto his disciples, Thus shall ye say unto them, What man among you, having a son, and he shall be standing out, and shall say, Father, open thy house that I may come in and sup with thee, will not say, Come in, my son; for mine is thine, and thine is mine?* Or what man is there *among* you, *who,* if his son ask bread, will give him a stone?" (JST Matthew 7:9; italics indicate changes to the KJV text).

Study Questions

1. The Sermon on the Mount is perhaps Jesus's greatest recorded sermon. What reasons can you give to support this statement?

2. What are the individual blessings associated with the Beatitudes, and what do those blessings mean to you?

3. What additional insights to the Lord's Prayer does Elder Talmage provide? How do you feel when you read the Lord's Prayer aloud?

CHAPTER 18

AS ONE HAVING AUTHORITY

Elder Talmage reviews the story of John the Baptist's imprisonment and death, as well as Jesus's discourse after some of John's disciples inquired whether Jesus was the Messiah.

In the Gospel of Matthew, the order of arrest, imprisonment, and death is told several chapters after John the Baptist sent a delegation to Jesus—giving the impression that John languished in prison for a significant amount of time. The time between events seems much shorter in Mark; therefore, John may have been imprisoned for only a relatively short time. The cause of John's imprisonment was his denunciation of Herod Antipas's wedding to Herodias, the former wife of his brother Herod Philip (Matthew 14:3–4; Mark 6:17–18; Luke 7:5; John 5).

According to Josephus, John the Baptist was put to death at the Herodian fortress Machaerus, located on the eastern shore of the Dead Sea. During the crucial days before John's beheading, Jesus testified of John's calling, perhaps intending to warn Herod or to help John's disciples understand the transition from following John to accepting Jesus as the Messiah. In that discourse, Jesus taught several thought-provoking truths about John. "But what went ye out for to see?" He asked. "A prophet? yea, I say unto you, and more than a prophet" (Matthew 11:9).

In this declaration, Jesus praised John in the most profound way. The reference to John as "more than a prophet" by the Lord Himself will forever stand as a memorial to him.

During Jesus's ministry, a number of notable women became His disciples. The term *disciple* in the New Testament is sometimes used in a general sense to mean "student follower" and sometimes in a specific sense to designate an Apostle. Luke portrays Mary, the mother of Christ, as His first disciple; she appears in Luke 1 and Acts 1, a witness of the birth of the Messiah and of the birth of His Church following His Resurrection. After Jesus's mother, Mary Magdalene may be the most recognizable name among the female disciples; she remained faithful to the Lord during His entire public ministry. According to a passing reference in Luke, Mary Magdalene was healed of demonic possession, and, as a result, she and others showed their gratitude by administering "unto him of their substance" (Luke 8:2–3).

We can easily overlook the important roles that women played in the Lord's ministry because the male names are so prominent. Typical of first-century practice in both Roman and Jewish cultures, the New Testament often highlights men. Nevertheless, several women are certainly noteworthy for their faith and devotion. Luke's phrase "ministered unto him" implies that three women in particular—Joanna, Susanna, and Mary Magdalene—gave financial and other support for Jesus in His travels and ministry.

SINCE 1915

Antipas and John the Baptist. Mark tells us that Herod Antipas, son of Herod the Great, sought out John, had him arrested and then put to death and that Antipas's wife, Herodias, and her daughter, Salome, were involved in the intrigue.

At first sorry to carry out his wife's demand, Antipas ultimately ordered the beheading of the Baptist. Jesus expressed his disdain of Antipas when he said, "Go ye, and tell that fox . . ." (Luke 13:32). Later, Jesus appeared before Herod Antipas during His own trial, but He refused to speak to him (Luke 23:7–11). The Apostle Matthew, or Levi, may have been employed by Antipas or his brother Philip. We know that Matthew was a customs collector in the region of Capernaum where tolls were collected from travelers entering Antipas's territory from Philip's territory (Matthew 9:9).

The healing of the centurion's son. The Gospel of Matthew recounts the healing of the centurion's servant: "Lord," the centurion said, "my servant lieth at home sick of the palsy, grievously tormented" (Matthew 8:6; cf. Luke 7:2). A nearly identical story is told in the Gospel of John, when it is a nobleman's son who is ill: "And there was a certain nobleman, whose son was sick at Capernaum" (John 4:46; cf. 4:49). The word translated as "servant" in the Gospel of Matthew can also mean "son," and in this case, Matthew, Luke, and John may have been relating the same story of an influential individual in Capernaum whose son was dying.

Mary Magdalene. Mary Magdalene, whose name in Hebrew or Aramaic was Miriam of Magdala, came from a thriving commercial fishing town on the western shore of the Sea of Galilee, north of Tiberias and southwest of Capernaum. We know little about Mary's background except that she had been healed from being possessed by evil spirits (Luke 8:2).

Along with Mary, Luke mentions Joanna and Susanna and states that these three women "ministered unto [Jesus] of their substance" (Luke 8:3) or that they provided Him assistance. This suggests a reciprocal relationship between Jesus and Mary Magdalene: He healed her, and she showed her gratitude by supporting Him in His ministry.

The Beelzebub accusation. In Matthew 12, Jesus is accused of healing through the power of Beelzebub. The most common interpretation of the title "Beelzebub" is "lord of the flies"— that is, Satan. When Jesus healed a man who could not speak or see (Matthew 12:22), some who witnessed the event wondered if Jesus were the Messiah who should come (Matthew 12:23). But the Pharisees immediately claimed that Jesus's healing power came from Beelzebub. Because there were so many witnesses, the Pharisees were forced to invent an explanation for the public healings, the only one that allowed them to admit that the healings were real and, at the same time, discredit the source.

JOSEPH SMITH'S TEACHINGS

Matthew 11:9–12. "How is it John was considered one of the greatest of prophets? Three things: First, he was trusted with a divine mission of preparing the way before the face of the Lord. [Who ever received such] trust before or since? No man. Second, he was trusted, and it was required at his hands to baptize the Son of Man. Who ever did that? Who had so great a privilege and glory [to lead the] Son of God into the waters of baptism, beholding the Holy Ghost in the sign of a dove? [The sign of the dove was] instituted before the creation. The Devil could not come in [the] sign of a dove. [The] Holy Ghost is a personage in the form of a personage. [He] does not confine [himself] to [the] form of a dove, but in [the] sign of a dove. No man holds the book [the Bible] more sacred than I do. Third, John at that time was the only legal administrator holding the keys of power, there was on earth" (Discourse, 29 January 1843, recorded by Willard Richards, as cited in Jackson, *Joseph Smith's Commentary,* 87 and 79, combined; see also Journal, December 1842–June 1844; Book 1, 21 December 1842–10 March 1843, The Joseph Smith Papers, accessed 21 February 2014, http://josephsmithpapers.org /paperSummary/journal-december-1842-june-1844-book-1-21 -december-1842-10-march-1843?p=162).

Matthew 9:14. "The spirit of Elias is to prepare the way for a greater revelation of God. [This] is the priesthood of Elias, or the priesthood that Aaron was ordained unto. And when God sends a man into the world to prepare for a greater work, [he] holds the keys of [the] power of Elias. It was called the doctrine of Elias even from the early ages of the world" (Wilford Woodruff Journal, 10 March 1844, Church History Library, The Church of Jesus Christ of Latter-day Saints, Salt Lake City, Utah).

JOSEPH SMITH TRANSLATION

A change in Matthew 11 reflects a clear doctrinal statement from the Joseph Smith Translation on the mission and role of Elias: *"But the days will come, when the violent shall have no power;* for all the prophets and the law prophesied, *that it should be thus* until John. *Yea, as many as have prophesied have foretold of these days.* And if ye will receive it, *verily he was the* Elias, *who* was for to come *and prepare all things"* (JST Matthew 11:13–15; italics indicate changes to the KJV text). A further change in Matthew also teaches about the calling of Elias: *"And again* I say unto you that Elias *has* come already, *concerning whom it is written, Behold I will send my messenger, and he shall prepare the way before me;* and they knew him not, *and* have done unto him whatsoever they listed. Likewise shall also the Son of man suffer of them" (JST Matthew 17:12; italics indicate changes to the KJV text).

STUDY QUESTIONS

1. Why did Herod Antipas both fear and respect John the Baptist?
2. What are the common elements in the miracles of healing discussed in this chapter?
3. How can we avoid seeking signs to build our faith?

CHAPTER 19

"HE SPAKE MANY THINGS UNTO THEM IN PARABLES"

One particularly important chapter from the Gospel of Matthew is Matthew 13, the first chapter devoted entirely to Jesus's parables (see also Matthew 25). According to Matthew, Jesus began teaching in parables because of the increasing opposition He faced. After the accusation that He healed by the power of Beelzebub, Jesus began to veil His teachings by using parables: "Because it is given unto you to know the mysteries of the kingdom of heaven, but to them it is not given" (Matthew 13:11). Jesus used parables to convey profound truth in simple terms that may be overlooked by those without "ears to hear" (Matthew 13:9). For this reason, Matthew, unlike any other Gospel author, gathered the parables together to give them focus and greater prominence.

The parables are told in an order that suggests linear development, an insight noted by the Prophet Joseph Smith (see below). The parables reach from the time of the disciples, expressed in the parable of the sower and the parable of the wheat and the tares, to modern times, expressed in several of the parables but particularly in the parable of the net cast into the sea.

The disciples sought an interpretation of only one of Jesus's parables, the parable of the wheat and the tares, or "the parable of the tares in the field" (Matthew 13:36). Jesus's response described a future apostasy when tares would infest the gospel field and the Apostles would be faced with leading the Church during those trying times.

SINCE 1915

The family of Jesus. Two verses in the New Testament explicitly mention Jesus's family members by name, and several other verses suggest that He had a number of brothers and sisters. According to Matthew and Mark, Jesus had at least four brothers and two sisters: "Is not this the carpenter's son? is not his mother called Mary? and his brethren, James, and Joses, and Simon, and Judas? And his sisters, are they not all with us?" (Matthew 13:55–56; Mark 6:3). These siblings were younger than Jesus and grew up with Him in Nazareth. His sisters' names are not known.

During Jesus's ministry, at least some of His brothers did not understand who He was: "For neither did his brethren believe in him" (John 7:5). Some of those same brothers were likely in the upper room with Jesus's mother and His disciples during the days following the Resurrection (Acts 1:14); His brother James was blessed with the privilege of seeing the resurrected Christ (1 Corinthians 15:7). Tradition holds that Jesus's brother James is the author of the Epistle of James, and His brother Jude (or Judas) is credited as the author of the Epistle of Jude.

Although some faith traditions dispute the claim that Joseph and Mary did not have children after she gave birth to Jesus, because of the belief in Mary's perpetual virginity, the simplest reading of the New Testament suggests that those mentioned as the brothers and sisters of Jesus were natural children of Mary and her husband, Joseph.

JOSEPH SMITH'S TEACHINGS

Matthew 13:1–3. "I shall now proceed to make some remarks from the sayings of the Savior, recorded in the 13th chapter of his gospel according to St. Matthew, which in my mind afford us as clear an understanding upon the important subject of the gathering as anything recorded in the Bible" ("To the Elders of the Church of the Latter Day Saints," *Messenger and Advocate,* December 1835, 225, as cited in Jackson, *Joseph Smith's Commentary,* 91).

Matthew 5:10–12. "Shall a man be considered bad when men speak evil of him? No: If a man stands and opposes the world of sin, he may expect all things arrayed against him" (Nauvoo Relief Society Minute Book, 31 August 1842, The Joseph Smith Papers, accessed 21 February 2014, http://josephsmithpapers.org /paperSummary/nauvoo-relief-society-minute-book?p=79).

Matthew 5:43–45. "While one portion of the human race are judging and condemning the other without mercy, the great parent of the universe looks upon the whole of the human family with a fatherly care, and paternal regard; he views them as his offspring; and without any of those contracted feelings that influence the children of men, causes '*his sun* to rise on the evil and the good, and sends *his rain* on the just and unjust'" ("Baptism for the Dead," *Times and Seasons,* 15 April 1842, 759).

STUDY QUESTIONS

1. What are the dangers of taking the analogies of the parables too far?

2. What truths do you see in Jesus's parables? How should these truths influence the way you teach the gospel?

3. How do the parables help you understand Jesus's message?

CHAPTER 20

"PEACE, BE STILL"

After the Sermon on the Mount, several important miracles occurred during a formative period in Jesus's ministry. These miracles seem to have had two different effects: they strengthened the faith of those already close to Jesus, and they increased opposition against Jesus as His opponents found offensive the way the miracle was performed or something that was said.

Some of Jesus's opponents were products of socially conservative villages in Galilee and Judea. Healings performed by Jesus challenged social standards built around ritual purity rules of "clean" and "unclean" found in the Torah. Originally, these rules applied to priests who served in the temple. Later, these rules were extended to others outside the temple.

Miracles from this time period include the stilling of the storm on the Sea of Galilee (Matthew 8:23–27), the healing of the man possessed with a legion of devils (Mark 5:1–19), the raising of Jairus's daughter (Matthew 9:18–19, 23–26), the healing of the woman with an issue of blood (Matthew 9:20–22), and the healing of the two men who were blind (Matthew 9:27–30).

Elder Talmage draws attention to the faith that is required to be healed and how that faith shapes and directs action. Jesus often said to those He blessed, "Thy faith hath made thee whole" (Mark 5:34). In this chapter, Elder Talmage seems to hint that the reason for some of the miracles was to demonstrate a cause-and-effect relationship between having faith and being healed. However, the fact that it remains a hint suggests his awareness that not all faithful people are healed and that these miracles are the exception rather than the norm. For the faithful, the miracles are something to contemplate as part of our own development and growth.

SINCE 1915

The hem of Jesus's garment. We know very little about the clothing Jesus wore during mortality. We do know that the woman with an issue of blood reached out and touched the hem of His robe. That "hem" was likely the fringes (Hebrew, *tzitzit*) that were attached to the edge of the Jewish prayer shawl and to the everyday clothing of Jewish males. The law of Moses mandated: "Make them fringes in the borders of their garments throughout their generations, and that they put upon the fringe of the borders a ribband of blue" (Numbers 15:38).

JOSEPH SMITH'S TEACHINGS

Matthew 8:28–34. "The great principle of happiness consists in having a body. The Devil has no body, and herein is his punishment. He is pleased when he can obtain the tabernacle of [a] man, and when cast out by the Savior, he asked to go into a herd of swine, showing that he would prefer a swine's body to having none. All beings who have bodies have power over those who have not. The Devil has no power over us, only as we permit him; the moment we revolt at anything which comes from God, the Devil takes power" (Discourse, 5 January 1841, recorded by William Clayton, as cited in Jackson, *Joseph Smith's Commentary*, 84; see also The Joseph Smith Papers, accessed 21 February 2014, http://josephsmithpapers.org/paperSummary /discourse-5-january-1841-as-reported-by-william-clayton?p=4).

JOSEPH SMITH TRANSLATION

Two minor changes in the Joseph Smith Translation confirm the idea that a connection exists between believing and being healed. First, "And Jesus went about all Galilee, teaching in their synagogues, and preaching the gospel of the kingdom, and healing all manner of sickness and all manner of *diseases* among the people *which believed on his name*" (JST Matthew 4:23; italics indicate changes to the KJV text). Second, "And great multitudes followed him; *and many believed on him* and he healed them there" (JST Matthew 19:2; italics indicate changes to the KJV text).

STUDY QUESTIONS

1. Why did the Lord *choose* His Apostles instead of merely relying on those who asked to join Him?
2. How do you feel as you read the story of Jesus stilling the storm?
3. What common elements or themes are found in the healing of Jarius's daughter and the unnamed woman who touched Jesus's hem?
4. Remember an occasion when you felt peace in your life and then ask yourself, "How can I experience that same feeling again?"

CHAPTER 21

THE APOSTOLIC MISSION, AND EVENTS RELATED THERETO

Latter-day Saint doctrine helps us understand that when Jesus sent His Apostles on a mission, they taught His new gospel and administered priesthood ordinances, a phrase not found in the New Testament. Their call to the mission (Matthew 10) is described in great detail, but little is reported about their return or their successes and failures.

Matthew reports five specifics of the Apostles' mission: (1) Jesus sent them to the "lost" within Israel but instructed them not to venture into Gentile or Samaritan cities; (2) they were to teach that the "kingdom of heaven is at hand"; (3) they were to use their priesthood to heal the sick, raise the dead, and cast out devils; (4) they were not to take with them money or food; and (5) they were to dust off their feet in a symbolic gesture against those who rejected them. The mission, as far as we are able to tell today, was to Galilee during a period of time when Jesus was also in Galilee. They were nearby, and they probably had communication with Jesus during their mission, but this was their first opportunity to teach the good news of the gospel on their own.

Their mission came at a time when the Twelve Apostles were being trained to lead the kingdom after Jesus's departure. By giving these early disciples so much authority, Jesus effectively trusted them with His full power. When they saw Jesus do the very things they were commanded to do, both before and after their missions, they received confidence to exercise the power they had been given.

Another story highlighted in this chapter of *Jesus the Christ* is the feeding of the five thousand, an event that is recounted in all four Gospels, including in an entire chapter in John.

John's account, now known as the bread of life discourse, gives several insights that are not found in the other accounts. In the synoptic Gospels, the main image to emerge from the stories is that of Jesus feeding Israel in much the same way that Moses fed Israel in the wilderness. In John, the story develops as some in the crowd are so impressed with Jesus's actions that they intend to "take him by force, to make him a king." In response to their actions, Jesus "departed again into a mountain himself alone" (John 6:15). The bread of life discourse is then given to those who persisted in seeking Jesus after He "departed" to be "alone." Jesus's fame spread because of a false belief that was founded on temporal rather than spiritual things: "Ye seek me, not because ye saw the miracles, but because ye did eat of the loaves, and were filled" (John 6:26).

This sermon, given at the synagogue in Capernaum after the feeding of the five thousand, is a study in contrasts between images that were familiar and comforting and images of things that were future, unfamiliar, and difficult to understand. For the faithful, the sermon includes some of Jesus's plainest teachings, such as His declaration, "I am the bread of life: he that cometh to me shall never hunger; and he that believeth on me shall never thirst" (John 6:35).

At first, the discourse was positive in tone, declaring what Jesus had come to achieve in His ministry. Near the end of the discourse, however, it took on a different tone when Jesus invoked the future symbols of the sacrament that would represent His flesh and blood: "Whoso eateth my flesh, and drinketh my blood, hath eternal life; and I will raise him up at the last day" (John 6:54). In retrospect, those symbols are easy to understand and embrace; but to those who had no context in which to understand them, they were difficult to accept, and the encounter became somewhat confrontational.

The end of the discourse reveals that Jesus invoked such strong symbols so His disciples would be forced to make a choice. As John reports, some of the disciples were indeed affected by the strong language: "Many therefore of his disciples, when they had heard this, said, This is an hard saying; who can hear it?" (John 6:60). As a result, "From that time many of his disciples went back, and walked no more with him" (John 6:66).

Jesus probed the Twelve, asking if they were also offended: "Then said Jesus unto the twelve, Will ye also go away?" (John 6:67). Peter responded in faith, "Lord, to whom shall we go? thou hast the words of eternal life" (John 6:68).

JOSEPH SMITH'S TEACHINGS

John 6:68. "The Savior has the words of Eternal life—nothing else can profit us" (Thomas Bullock Report, 12 May 1844, as cited in Ehat and Cook, *Words of Joseph Smith*, 365).

JOSEPH SMITH TRANSLATION

Chapter 6 of the Gospel of John is treated extensively in chapter 21 of *Jesus the Christ*. One noteworthy change, illuminating how the Father and Son work together and testify of each other, echoes earlier changes with similar themes, such as the way prophets, and even the Father, had plainly testified of the Son. This change, added to the sermon known as the discourse on the bread of life, reads: "No man can come to me, except *he doeth the will of my* Father *who hath* sent me. *And this is the will of him who hath sent me, that ye receive the Son; for the Father beareth record of him; and he who receiveth the testimony, and doeth the will of him who sent me,* I will raise up *in the resurrection of the just*" (JST John 6:44; italics indicate changes to the KJV text). This change typifies many corrections made by the Prophet Joseph Smith to the Bible text—changes that speak of greater harmony between the work of the Father and the Son and ultimately between the work of the Son and His Old Testament prophets.

STUDY QUESTIONS

1. Jesus taught and then fed two very large multitudes. What reasons do the Gospels give for Jesus's decision to feed the five thousand and the four thousand?

2. Why was the doctrine taught in the bread of life discourse so challenging for many of Jesus's disciples?

3. How do you remain faithful when faced with doctrinal, historical, or cultural issues you do not understand? Why is it important to respond the way the disciples did: "Lord, to whom shall we go? thou hast the words of eternal life. And we believe and are sure that thou art that Christ, the Son of the living God"? (John 6:68–69).

CHAPTER 22

A PERIOD OF
DARKENING OPPOSITION

Elder Talmage sets the stage for Jesus's final year by highlighting His confrontation with the Pharisees about "the tradition of the elders" (350–54). The encounter foreshadows His last confrontation with the chief priests in Jerusalem, leading to Jesus's arrest and execution.

According to Matthew's order of events, Jesus traveled to the coastal cities of Tyre and Sidon, where He and the disciples encountered a woman who begged for Jesus to heal her daughter from illness. As told in Matthew, the story is poignant as Jesus uses language typical of Jewish descriptions of Gentiles: "It is not meet to take the children's bread, and to cast it to dogs" (Matthew 15:26). Commentators have long wrestled with these words because they seem to imply that Jesus referred to the woman as a dog, the way a Jewish male might refer to a Gentile woman.

Matthew tells the story for a very specific reason, unaware that it might challenge our modern sensibilities. The woman responds in faith to what appears to be a denial of her request: "Truth, Lord: yet the dogs eat of the crumbs which fall from their masters' table" (Matthew 15:27). In return, Jesus commends her hopeful statement: "O woman, great is thy faith: be it unto thee even as thou wilt" (Matthew 15:28).

The story continues as Jesus returns to the region of the Sea of Galilee where He is greeted by a large multitude, who brought many who were afflicted for Jesus to heal. We see a reflective Lord who had "compassion on the multitude, because they continue with me now three days" (Matthew 15:32).

This time the multitude numbered approximately four thousand individuals, and once again He fed them. The account of the bread of life discourse notes that many of Jesus's disciples ceased to follow Him (John 6:66); perhaps the number four thousand can be interpreted to mean that about one-fifth of His followers left.

The story in Matthew directs the narrative from an increasingly compassionate leader who feeds His followers to one who ultimately gives His life for His flock.

SINCE 1915

Simon Peter. Jesus's chief Apostle is identified in the New Testament by several different names, including his birth name Simon (pronounced *Shimôn*); Cephas (*Kefas*), a name given to him by Jesus; and Peter, the English equivalent of the Greek translation of Cephas. We commonly refer to the chief Apostle by his nickname Peter, meaning "rock" or "stone." The New Testament preserves Peter's father's name, Jona (John); his brother's name, Andrew; and the facts that Peter was married and that his mother-in-law lived with him in Capernaum (Matthew 8:14).

Tyre and Sidon. The two coastal cities of Tyre and Sidon lay beyond the boundaries of Galilee and were inhabited by Gentiles. Jesus's visit to these two cities was the first recorded instance of His going beyond Galilee, the Decapolis, or Judea. His interactions in the region with a Gentile woman were noteworthy (Matthew 15:21–31).

Dogs. When Matthew recorded Jesus's words, "It is not meet to take the children's bread, and to cast it to dogs" (Matthew 15:26), he used the diminutive form of the word *dog,* indicating a house dog rather than a larger dog. However, Jesus spoke Aramaic, and we have no way of knowing if Matthew used the correct word. Given the context, scholars have speculated that Jesus may have made the statement to help His disciples see that a Gentile woman could express great faith. Following standard social practices of the day, the disciples had "besought" Jesus to send the woman away. Instead, He helped them see the future of the kingdom—a kingdom that included women and Gentiles.

JOSEPH SMITH'S TEACHINGS

Matthew 16:18. "Jesus in his teaching says: 'Upon this rock I will build my church; and the gates of hell shall not prevail against it.' What rock? Revelation" (Discourse, 22 January 1843, recorded by Wilford Woodruff, as cited in Jackson, *Joseph Smith's Commentary,* 99).

JOSEPH SMITH TRANSLATION

A change to the bread of life discourse focuses on what it means to be a disciple of Christ: "No man can come to me, except *he doeth the will of my* Father *who* hath sent me. *And this is the will of him who hath sent me, that ye receive the Son; for the Father beareth record of him; and he who receiveth the testimony, and doeth the will of him who sent me,* I will raise up *in the resurrection of the just"* (JST John 6:44; italics indicate changes to the KJV text). This addition connects some of the precepts in the bread of life discourse with Jesus's teachings in John 5:29 about the first and second resurrection.

Study Questions

1. What events and conflicts can you identify that led up to the rejection of Jesus in Galilee and Jerusalem?
2. How had the disciples been prepared to answer the question, "Whom say ye that I am"?
3. Share with someone your feelings about who Christ is and then think about your experience. What thoughts come to your mind about how you can share your testimony more often and with deeper conviction?

CHAPTER 23

THE TRANSFIGURATION

Not far from the site where Jesus ascended Mount Hermon with three of His disciples—and there experienced events described by three of the evangelists—is a Roman city named Caesarea Philippi, built by Herod Phillip, one of Herod the Great's sons. In Roman times, the area had several pagan temples, including one dedicated to the Roman emperor Augustus; another to Pan, the Greek god of the wild and protector of shepherds and their flocks; and several burial niches.

The site is remarkable for several reasons. The headwaters of the River Jordan begin from a fissure in the ground and literally rise up to create a fairly significant river. In the first century, the headwaters began in the mouth of a cave at the foot of a limestone hillside; earthquakes over the centuries have caused the headwaters to move several hundred feet away from the mouth of the cave. The site is also noteworthy because it was not typical for Jesus to visit such outwardly pagan shrines or locations that were

devoted to the care of the ancestral dead. It is as if two themes—
Gentiles and death—were being interwoven into the fabric of the
story.

While at or near Caesarea Philippi, Jesus asked His disciples,
"Whom say ye that I am?" (Matthew 16:15). Jesus was not taking
an opinion poll of what people were saying about Him; He was
laying a foundation for a conversation He wanted to have with
the disciples.

Peter answered in a way that evoked great praise from the
Lord: "And Simon Peter answered and said, Thou art the Christ,
the Son of the living God" (Matthew 16:16). What follows is a
celebration of months, even two or more years, of training. The
disciples were now fully prepared to accept Jesus for who He was,
"the Christ," or the Messiah who would redeem Israel. However,
they did not fully understand what that meant—that Jesus would
suffer, die, and be resurrected.

Much attention has been paid to the wordplay on Peter's
name when the Lord said to Peter, "Blessed art thou, Simon Bar-
jona: for flesh and blood hath not revealed it unto thee, but my
Father which is in heaven. And I say also unto thee, That thou art
Peter, and upon this rock I will build my church; and the gates of
hell shall not prevail against it" (Matthew 16:17–18).

The name Peter (Greek, *petros*) means "rock," and the
word *rock* in Matthew 16:17–18 is from the same Greek word.
Commentators have long recognized that Jesus was explicitly
drawing attention to the idea that Peter was a rock and that He
planned to build His church upon the rock of belief in Him:
"Thou art the Christ, the Son of the living God." Although Peter's
testimony was the foundation rock of the new faith, Peter was
also called as the leader of that new faith. To him would be given
the keys of the kingdom to lead and direct and go forward in

Jesus's name: "And I will give unto thee the keys of the kingdom of heaven" (Matthew 16:19). The wordplay was a subtle reminder of Peter's calling and authority to lead the believers in Jesus Christ.

Following the experiences at Caesarea Philippi, Jesus singled out Peter, James, and John, who had over the past months emerged as leaders amongst the Twelve, for a private experience that would shape their lives and the lives of the early members of the Church.

As preserved in the Gospels, the accounts of what happened on the Mount of Transfiguration are quite brief. The Mount of Transfiguration is described as such because Jesus was visibly changed, or transfigured, before the eyes of Peter, James, and John. The Greek word that describes the changes to Jesus's appearance is the root word for the English word *metamorphosis.* Thus, Jesus changed or experienced metamorphosis before their eyes (Matthew 17:2).

The precise changes in His personage are not described, but the connection with Caesarea Philippi, where Peter testified that Jesus was the Christ, implies that somehow this reality was conveyed to the disciples in visual form. During their time on the mount, the disciples also heard the voice of God the Father confirm His trust and faith in His son: "This is my beloved Son, in whom I am well pleased; hear ye him" (Matthew 17:5). Restoration scripture and teachings reveal that the keys promised to Peter were, in fact, transferred to Peter, James, and John on the mount.

At its core, the Mount of Transfiguration is the moment when the faith of the disciples became certain—when what they believed became for them a sure knowledge and a point from which they could go forth and lead the kingdom. For a brief moment, they saw Jesus as He really was—the divine Son of Man described in Daniel 7.

SINCE 1915

"**I will build my church.**" These words have caused a great deal of discussion among scholars because they imply that Jesus formed a church and that He intended to start a religion that would be separate from Judaism. The questions raised by scholars are answered through Restoration scriptures and teachings, which confirm that Jesus did establish a church and prepared leaders for it. From a Restoration perspective, we can note three important moments in His ministry as Jesus prepared leaders to guide the Church after His death.

First, Jesus and His disciples baptized people using an ordinance that was usually reserved for individuals who wished to convert to Judaism. The requirement of baptism recalled proselyte baptisms and signaled that those baptized were entering into a new faith or covenant.

Second, Jesus organized His followers into groups, such as of the Twelve Apostles and the Seventy, and He sent them on missions to declare His word.

Finally, Jesus's disciples were given priesthood authority to teach and bless in Jesus's name, clearly separate from the priesthood the Levites held by virtue of birthright.

Before His death, Jesus began speaking of the future kingdom as a "church."

JOSEPH SMITH'S TEACHINGS

Matthew 16:19. "Now the great and grand secret of the whole matter, and the sum and bonum of the whole subject that is lying before us, consists in obtaining the powers of the Holy

Priesthood. For him to whom these keys are given, there is no difficulty in obtaining a knowledge of facts in relation to the salvation of the children of men, both as well for the dead as for the living. . . . This, therefore, is the sealing and binding power, and, in one sense of the word, the keys of the kingdom, which consist of the key of knowledge" ("Letter from Joseph Smith, Nauvoo, September 6, 1842," *Times and Seasons,* 1 October 1842, 935; see also Doctrine and Covenants 128:11, 14).

JOSEPH SMITH TRANSLATION

The Joseph Smith Translation changes to Mark 9 have caused confusion for some because the changed verse seems to restate what is said in the other Gospels by correcting the idea that Elijah was on the Mount of Transfiguration. The JST seems to imply that instead of Elijah, John the Baptist was on the mount: "And there appeared unto them Elias with Moses, *or in other words, John the Baptist and Moses:* and they were talking with Jesus" (JST Mark 9:4; italics indicate changes to the KJV text).

We cannot fully know what Joseph Smith intended, but if we combine Matthew's and Luke's accounts with Mark 9:4 in the JST, the possibility arises that all three—Elijah, John the Baptist as Elias, and Moses—were on the mount. The LDS Bible Dictionary interprets the passage in this way, that Elijah, Moses, and John the Baptist all ministered to the disciples while they were on the mount.

STUDY QUESTIONS

1. Elder Talmage provides a powerful discussion of the events that took place on the Mount of Transfiguration. What events are most important for understanding the restoration of the priesthood in the latter days?

2. What is the significance of the Father's words "Hear ye him" (JST Matthew 3:46) for the disciples and for you?

3. What can you do to hear Christ's voice more this week than you did last week?

CHAPTER 24

FROM SUNSHINE
TO SHADOW

One touching story from this time period occurred when a group of children were brought to Jesus to be blessed: "And they brought unto him also infants, that he would touch them: but when his disciples saw it, they rebuked them" (Luke 18:15). When the disciples rebuked the parents of the children, or possibly the children themselves, the disciples were following the social customs of the day. Children were not allowed direct interaction with an adult, particularly not a great healer and leader such as Jesus was.

The disciples likely thought their actions were appropriate and that they were doing what anyone in their situation would have done. But Jesus paused to bless the children: "Jesus called them unto him, and said, Suffer little children to come unto me, and forbid them not: for of such is the kingdom of God" (Luke 18:16). The story follows the theme of the parables in Luke 15: God cares for even the least among us. Jesus gave His individual attention, which would have been considered unusual in that era, to make a point and teach a principle.

This chapter of *Jesus the Christ* also emphasizes the need to be like a little child: "Verily I say unto you, Except ye be converted, and become as little children, ye shall not enter into the kingdom of heaven. Whosoever therefore shall humble himself as this little child, the same is greatest in the kingdom of heaven" (Matthew 18:3–4). First-century cultural norms called for little children to be quiet and not to draw attention to themselves. They were also required to work for the common good of the family. In many respects, the role of the child was similar to the role of a faithful servant. When Jesus encouraged His followers to be like little children, He may also have been subtly rebuking adults who seek attention and praise.

SINCE 1915

Money in the New Testament. One of the challenges for the modern student of the New Testament arises because references to money have been translated into seventeenth-century English terms; the words in the original language of the New Testament accounts are not used. For example, in the King James Version, references are made to a "penny," a "farthing," and a "mite" (Luke 20:24; Matthew 10:29; Mark 12:42). The most common monetary references in the Greek New Testament are to the denarius (Roman), the drachma (Greek), and the lepton (Greek). The denarius and drachma were the most commonly used units of money, and a typical wage for a full-grown, able-bodied adult male would have been about eight drachmae or denarii for a full day's work. The amount would be less if that person were disabled, young, or female. The lepton was worth about 1/32 of a drachma.

A similar approach is used for measurements of weight and volume. For example, in John 2:6, the KJV uses *firkins* to translate the original Greek term *meteras*, meaning "measures." Two or three measures, or firkins, would be the equivalent of about forty liters, or ten American gallons.

Talents and pence. Elder Talmage provides a 1915 monetary equivalent for two debts, the first sum equaling "over nine and a quarter millions of dollars" and the second "about fifteen dollars" (396–97). The equivalents today, a century later, are estimated to be more than $213 million for the first debt and $346 for the second.

JOSEPH SMITH TRANSLATION

A change made in Matthew 16 nearly doubles the content of the original verse and gives a very precise definition of discipleship: "*And now for a man to take up his cross, is to deny himself from all ungodliness, and from every worldly lust, and keep my commandments. Break not my commandments, for to save your lives;* for whosoever will save his life *in this world,* shall lose it *in the world to come;* and whosoever will lose his life *in this world* for my sake shall find it *in the world to come*" (JST Matthew 16:25; italics indicate changes to the KJV text).

Several of the changes to the Gospel of Mark also treat the topic of discipleship—its definition and its blessings, as well as the consequences that come to those who choose not to be disciples. The JST adds a significant amount of context to a familiar passage from Mark 9 asserting that family members or associates who offend believers will be punished for their actions: "*Therefore* if thy hand offend thee, cut it off: *or if thy brother offend thee, and confess not, and forsake not, he shall be cut off.* It is better for thee to enter into life maimed, than having two hands to go into hell;

for it is better for thee to enter into life without thy brother, than for thee and thy brother to be cast into hell; into the fire that never shall be quenched." In the changes made to Mark 9:45, the same consequences apply to leaders who go astray: "And *again,* if thy foot offend thee, cut it off: *for he that is thy standard, by whom thou walkest, if he become a transgressor, he shall be cut off*" (JST Mark 9:43–45; italics indicate changes to the KJV text).

The JST then admonishes: "*Therefore, let every man stand, or fall by himself, and not for another; or not trusting another. Seek unto my Father, and it shall be done in that very moment what ye shall ask, if ye ask in faith, believing that ye shall receive*" (JST Mark 9:46; italics indicate changes to the KJV text). Because family members may offend and because some who are examples among us may fall, the JST recommends that we stand by ourselves and rely on the Father for our example. These changes to the Gospel of Mark reflect the difficulties of conversion and the challenge conversion created for Jewish families of that day.

Study Questions

1. In what ways can you deepen your relationship with the Lord through prayer, study, and worship at church meetings or at the temple?
2. Why are children a model of perfect discipleship?
3. Take an opportunity to observe a group of children and ponder this question: "Why did Jesus ask me to be like them?"

CHAPTER 25

JESUS AGAIN
IN JERUSALEM

One of the central stories of this part of Jesus's ministry is His visit to Jerusalem to celebrate the Feast of Tabernacles (also called Sukkot). The visit is recorded mostly in John 7–8, but portions of John 9 and 10 may also have occurred during this visit. At the beginning of the story, John informs his readers that Jesus's life would be in danger if He traveled to Jerusalem to participate in the feast. The Feast of Tabernacles took place in late September or early October and focused on remembering Israel's sojourn in the wilderness.

Once again Jesus's religious devotions were interrupted when, upon His arrival in Jerusalem, He was discovered and confronted about His identity and about a healing that took place on the Sabbath. The encounter between Jesus and His opponents quickly turned hostile, and apparently some pressed Him to make a claim as to whether He considered Himself to be the Messiah. Clearly, John's warning that Jesus's life would be in danger in Jerusalem was merited. But the Feast of Tabernacles was not the right time for Jesus to give His life. Elder Talmage draws attention to the element of testimony and how it was a time for the people to choose whether they would accept Jesus as Messiah (400–402).

The crowning moment of the discourse in John 7–8 is the dramatic conclusion, where Jesus openly testifies, "Verily, verily, I say unto you, Before Abraham was, I am" (John 8:58). One of the difficulties with this verse is that we must rely on a translation of Jesus's words, and neither English nor Greek accurately conveys what He said in Aramaic. We know from the response of the crowd that some considered His words blasphemous: "Then took they up stones to cast at him" (John 8:59). To provoke such a reaction when He said, "I am," He must have been pronouncing the divine name YHWH, or Yahweh, meaning "I am."

The English, which here accurately reflects the Greek, is ambiguous, and if the wording is taken literally, Jesus apparently said, "Before Abraham was, Yahweh," giving us a sentence that seems to lack a finite verb. The question then becomes whether Jesus meant to say, "Before Abraham was, I am (or was) Yahweh" or "Before Abraham was, Yahweh is (or was)." Some of His listeners clearly thought He was declaring that He was indeed Yahweh, the God of the Old Testament, and many Christians read the verse that way. For the faithful believers in Jesus among the crowd, the statement signaled what they had always hoped—that Jesus was the very God of the Old Testament, who was called Yahweh and whose name is sometimes transliterated as *Jehovah* today. One of the names of Jehovah is I AM.

At the feast, Jesus also declares, "If any man thirst, let him come unto me, and drink"; He offers them "living water" (John 7:37–38). Later, He proclaims, "I am the light of the world"

(John 9:5). Both light and water are important symbols of this important feast.

A short narrative interrupts the larger discourse of John 7–8: the scandalous story of the woman who had been caught in the very act of committing adultery. Jesus's enemies want Him to pass sentence on her (John 8:1–11), thereby setting up a dilemma: If Jesus calls for the woman's condemnation, He is setting Himself up as a judge, a power that He does not have according to Jewish law and custom. If He does not condemn her, His enemies may accuse Him of disregard for the law.

Only with great difficulty can we imagine an answer that would be acceptable to Jesus's followers and to His enemies. In the end, He avoided passing judgment and instead called upon the sinless among the group to stone the woman on the spot. The story speaks to the mercy of Jesus, who, when given an opportunity to pass judgment upon what appears to be the most obvious of sins, Jesus declined to do so and encouraged the woman, "Neither do I condemn thee: go, and sin no more" (John 8:11). JST John 8:11 adds, "And the woman glorified God from that hour, and believed on his name."

SINCE 1915

Jewish holidays. The Jewish festival calendar is enormously different from our modern cycle of holidays, so reading about feasts and holy days in the New Testament can be confusing. The principal Jewish holidays mentioned in the New Testament are Passover (*Pesach;* Matthew 26:17), New Year (*Rosh Hashanah;* John 5:1), the Day of Atonement (*Yom Kippur;* Acts 27:9), the Feast of Dedication (*Hanukkah;* John 10:22), the Feast of Tabernacles (*Sukkot;* John 7:1–52), and Pentecost, or the Feast of Weeks (*Shavuot;* Acts 2:1). These holidays were sacred to the Jews of

Jesus's day, including to Jesus and His disciples; many of their trips to Jerusalem were for the purpose of celebrating one of these feasts or holidays.

The feasts focused on two major themes, the Jerusalem temple and Israel's wandering in the wilderness. When Jewish Christians eventually separated from Judaism, they continued to celebrate Passover in the form of Easter, but the majority of Christians began celebrating Easter on a different day because of a different way of calculating Easter's exact date.

The Pool of Siloam. Based on what he learned from studying Protestant scholars, Elder Talmage provides detailed information about the Pool of Siloam (421). Countless pilgrims and tourists have visited the site at the end of Hezekiah's Tunnel, believing it to be the first-century Pool of Siloam mentioned in the New Testament (John 9:7). In 2004, a rock-cut pool was discovered on the southern slope of the City of David, located outside the walls of the Old City. This surprising discovery showed that the Hezekiah's Tunnel site dated instead to the Byzantine period (late antiquity and medieval periods) and revealed what the true first-century pool looked like and where it was located. This discovery is one among many that have brought us closer to the first-century world of Jesus since Elder Talmage wrote *Jesus the Christ.*

His brethren. John reports that Jesus's brothers confronted Him just before the Feast of Tabernacles: "His brethren therefore said unto him, Depart hence, and go into Judea, that thy disciples also may see the works that thou doest. For there is no man that doeth any thing in secret, and he himself seeketh to be known openly. If thou do these things, shew thyself to the world. *For neither did his brethren believe in him*" (John 7:3–5; emphasis added). John highlights the dynamics inside Jesus's family, with some doubting Jesus's call and messianic claims. Later, the record shows that Jesus's family came to be numbered among the believers (Acts 1:14).

The adulterous woman. Elder Talmage notes the scholarly debate regarding the story of the woman caught in adultery (422; cf. John 8:1–11). By 1915, some scholars were questioning its authenticity because, they claimed, the language of the story is not representative of John's own language and it interrupts the flow of the narrative (John 7–9).

Advances in the study of the New Testament, including the discovery of earlier manuscripts since *Jesus the Christ* was written, indicate that the story of the woman taken in adultery (John 8:1–11) was almost certainly added to the Gospel of John after the Gospel was originally written. That is not sufficient reason, however, to doubt the story's antiquity or authenticity. Although the oldest manuscripts of the New Testament do not place the story at John 8:1, other teachings of Jesus, now referred to as the *agrapha*, also were not included in the Gospels. One example is found in the teachings of Paul: "I have shewed you all things, how that so labouring ye ought to support the weak, and to remember the words of the Lord Jesus, how he said, It is more blessed to give than to receive" (Acts 20:35). The number of Jesus's sayings must have been rather large, so we should not be surprised that all of them are not included in the Gospels. John himself said, "There are also many other things which Jesus did, the which if they should be written every one, I suppose that even the world itself could not contain the books that should be written" (John 21:25). Fortunately, this poignant story has been preserved, even if it might have been placed incorrectly.

JOSEPH SMITH'S TEACHINGS

John 8:56. "It will be noticed that according to Paul [Galatians 3:8], the gospel was preached to Abraham. We would like to be informed in what name the gospel was then preached, whether it was in the name of Christ or some other name. If in any other name, was it the gospel? And if it was the gospel, and that preached in the name of Christ, had it any ordinances? If not, was it the gospel? And if it had, what were they? Our friends may say, perhaps, that there were never any ordinances except those of offering sacrifices, before the coming of Christ, and that it could not be possible for the gospel to have been administered while the sacrifices of blood were. But we will recollect, that Abraham offered sacrifice and notwithstanding this, had the gospel preached to him. That the offering of sacrifice was only to point the mind forward to Christ we infer from these remarkable words of his to the Jews, 'Your father Abraham rejoiced to see my day: and he saw it, and was glad' [John 8:56]. So, then, because the ancients offered sacrifice it did not hinder their hearing the gospel; but served, as we said before, to open their eyes and enabled them to look forward to the time of the coming of the Savior, and to rejoice in his redemption" ("The Elders of the Church in Kirtland, to Their Brethren Abroad," *Evening and Morning Star,* March 1834, 143, as cited in Jackson, *Joseph Smith's Commentary,* 173–74).

JOSEPH SMITH TRANSLATION

In a change to an oft-quoted verse from the sermon delivered at the Feast of Tabernacles, the Joseph Smith Translation greatly clarifies what is otherwise a very difficult verse to interpret: "But this spake he of the Spirit, which they that believe on him should receive: for the Holy Ghost was *promised unto them who believe after* that Jesus was glorified" (John 7:39; italics indicate changes to the KJV text). The change may appear minor at first, but in the original, the verse reads, "for the Holy Ghost was *not* yet given" (emphasis added). This clarification removes the difficult words and connects the coming of the Holy Ghost to a promise that Jesus made to His disciples.

STUDY QUESTIONS

1. What do you consider to be Jesus's greatest parable from the ones that are discussed in chapter 25 of *Jesus the Christ*?
2. In this chapter, what evidence is given concerning Jesus's own religious practices?
3. Think of a time when someone spoke evil of you when you had done the right thing. How were you able not to be offended so you could truly forgive the person who said evil things about you?
4. How can you avoid hurting the feelings of others unnecessarily?

CHAPTER 26

OUR LORD'S MINISTRY
IN PEREA AND JUDEA

Elder Talmage reviews the story of the Seventy, whom Jesus called and sent forth to preach the gospel. Following their return, Jesus met "a certain lawyer" (Luke 10:25). The conversation between them introduces one of Jesus's best-known stories, the parable of the good Samaritan (Luke 10:30–37).

In this parable, Jesus tells the story of a Jew who fell among thieves and was beaten, robbed, and left to die. As the story unfolds, a priest comes upon the wounded man and passes by him. The next person to come upon the unfortunate man was a Levite. He too passes by without rendering aid. Jesus's listeners may have expected the next person to come along to be an Israelite; the threefold grouping of priest, Levite, and Israelite was common. Surprisingly, instead of an Israelite, a Samaritan, an enemy of Jews, appears on the scene; and, in the story's twist, the distressed Jew found help from a generous Samaritan rather than from his own countrymen.

The parable was obviously directed at Jews who could not imagine that a Samaritan could do anything good, especially toward a Jew. A similar story is found in the Old Testament, where a group of Samaritans care for Jewish victims of a battle (2 Chronicles 28:8–15, especially v. 15).

This parable offers a wider perspective on righteousness, suggesting that God sees the broader view and not simply the good or bad acts of the covenant people (the Jews) and that God also acknowledges the good acts of people who are not of the covenant (the Samaritans).

Elder Talmage then reviews the story of Martha and Mary; discusses prayer; gives three other parables—the friend at midnight, the foolish rich man, and the barren fig tree; heals a woman on the Sabbath; and responds to threats from Herod Antipas.

The chapter ends on a solemn note, "It cannot be that a prophet perish out of Jerusalem," which causes Jesus to weep for Jerusalem and its inhabitants (Luke 13:33–35).

JOSEPH SMITH TRANSLATION

The Joseph Smith Translation contains three changes, two to the Gospel of Luke and one to the Gospel of Mark, that appear to reach out to the disciples who have been faithful in following the Lord. Here, the Lord confirms the calling of His disciples and His Father's awareness of their needs:

"For all these things do the nations of the world seek after: and your Father *who is in heaven* knoweth that ye have need of these things. *And ye are sent unto them to be their ministers, and the labourer is worthy of his hire; for the law saith, that a man shall not muzzle the ox that treadeth out the corn*" (JST Luke 12:30; italics indicate changes to the KJV text).

A change in Mark also defines what the twelve disciples had

committed to do: "*Therefore deny yourselves of these, and be not ashamed of me.* Whosoever shall be ashamed of me and of my words in this adulterous and sinful generation; of him also shall the Son of man be ashamed, when he cometh in the glory of his Father with the holy angels. *And they shall not have part in that resurrection when he cometh. For verily I say unto you, that he shall come; and he that layeth down his life for my sake and the gospel's, shall come with him, and shall be clothed with his glory, in the cloud, on the right hand of the Son of Man*" (JST Mark 8:38; italics indicate changes to the KJV text).

STUDY QUESTIONS

1. What lessons can you draw from the parable of the good Samaritan about the relationship between the love for God and love for neighbor?

2. What do Jesus's teachings about the compassion of the Samaritan (the enemy of the Jewish man) inform us about our "enemies" in our families, neighborhoods, congregations, or across the world?

3. Why do we sometimes limit forgiveness, compassion, and love for others? Why is it natural for us to stereotype groups of people? How does this parable question stereotypes?

CHAPTER 27

CONTINUATION OF THE PEREAN AND JUDEAN MINISTRY

Some of Jesus's most notable parables come from this portion of His ministry, and several of them deserve our focused attention and prayerful consideration. Luke 15 contains three parables, each one documenting a different type of loss. The parables relate the story of a lost coin, the story of a lost sheep, and the story of lost sons, sometimes referred to in the singular as the parable of the prodigal son. The emphasis of the parables, as is often discussed, is on the *search* and the *joy* when the coin, the sheep, and the son are found.

In the first two parables, the lost item is rather small in comparison to other things but has great value of its own. The coin, for example, when compared to great wealth, is rather small, its value little more than the price of a loaf of bread. To the poor woman, however, the coin had great worth.

In the story of the lost sheep, the logical action would be to stay and guard the ninety-nine rather than leave the flock unguarded and go in search of the one. But Jesus was obviously drawing attention to the inherent value of "the one."

The third parable in the collection is usually viewed as a parable about the son who was prodigal (or wastefully extravagant), but anciently it was viewed as a parable about two equally unwise sons, one who left and squandered his inheritance and one who remained and complained that he was not given enough attention. In the context of the parables of the lost coin and lost sheep, this parable teaches the powerful lesson that the Father loves both of the unwise sons—the one who returned, implying that he repented of his ways, and the one who remained but who lost sight of what mattered most.

Equally powerful is the parable of the rich man and Lazarus (Luke 16:19–31). This parable contains the only individual with a name in all of Jesus's parables: Lazarus.

Lazarus is a poor man who begs at the gates of a wealthy man. Both men die, and the rich man finds himself separated from those in "Abraham's bosom" (Luke 16:22), the haven of the blessed. At first, it may appear that this parable is about the division in the world of the spirits, but the story is focused instead on the reversal of rewards. The rich man, whose sins are not specified, finds himself cursed, whereas Lazarus, whose good deeds are not specified, finds himself blessed.

What did the rich man do to earn a curse, and what did Lazarus do to earn a blessing? These may be the questions we should ask in seeking to understand this parable. Could it be that, in determining the fate of those who enter the world of spirits, God uses criteria that are not readily apparent to mortals? Those whom the world sees as blessed and prosperous may not be blessed in the hereafter, whereas those who are rejected by the world and who suffer and beg may find themselves in glorious circumstances in the hereafter. This type of parable helps disciples look at people's hearts rather than on outward appearances.

A parable discussed in this chapter of *Jesus the Christ* focuses on counting the cost of discipleship. Followers of Christ must build on a sure and solid foundation. This parable, however, asks the disciple to consider what needs to happen even before the foundation is laid: "For which of you, intending to build a tower, sitteth not down first, and counteth the cost, whether he have sufficient to finish it?" (Luke 14:28).

The intent of this parable may be to prepare the disciples for the loss of their Lord, a cost they would have to face in building their tower of faith. Elder Talmage draws attention to the fact that being a disciple of Christ requires complete, "self-sacrificing devotion" (452–53).

SINCE 1915

The eye of a needle. Elder Talmage debates the various possibilities of the meaning of the words, "It is easier for a camel to go through the eye of a needle, than for a rich man to enter into the kingdom of God" (Matthew 19:24) (478). One common suggestion is that scribes mistakenly wrote the word for *camel* when Jesus meant *rope*. The suggestion goes back to Cyril of Alexandria (ca. 444–376 BC), who thought that Greek *kamelos* was mistaken for *kamilos,* or "rope." The interchange of the two words has not been discovered in any ancient manuscripts of the Bible and is largely a conjecture that has been made both anciently and recently.

Another possibility suggested that the "eye of a needle" was the name of a gate in the ancient wall of Jerusalem. The suggestion was that this gate was very small and that to pass through it, a camel would need to kneel down, and all the goods it was carrying would have to be removed. No such gate existed, and the reference to it is of very late origin.

This adage comes after the encounter of Jesus with the rich young man who seemed unable to give up his possessions. Jesus tells His followers that if men "will forsake all things for my sake," only then can they hope to enter into the kingdom of God (JST Matthew 19:26). Man cannot save himself: "With men this is impossible; but with God all things are possible" (Matthew 19:26).

Children. The command to be like little children may conjure up images of childish or infantile behavior. Jesus, however, took notice of little children and their attributes of humility and innocence. Ancient authors rarely extolled the virtues of little children. One of the many insights that the Gospels provide about Jesus Christ is that He showed great care for and interest in children.

JOSEPH SMITH'S TEACHINGS

Luke 15:1–32. "What is the rule of interpretation? Just no interpretation at all, understood precisely as it reads. I have a key by which I understand the scripture: I inquire what was the question which drew out the answer. . . . First dig up the root. What drew the saying out of Jesus? Pharisees and scribes murmured: 'This man receiveth sinners, and eateth with them.' This is the key word—to answer the murmuring and questioning of Sadducees and Pharisees: 'Is this man as great as he pretends to be and eats with publicans and sinners?' 'This man receiveth sinners.' He spoke this parable: 'What man of you, having a hundred sheep and a hundred Sadducees and Pharisees . . . ?' 'If you Pharisees and Sadducees are in the sheepfold, I have no mission for you. [I am] sent to look up sheep that are lost. [I] will back them up and make joy in heaven, hunting after a few individuals, laying

[them] on [my] shoulder, one publican you despise, one piece of silver, the piece which was lost. Joy is found [in the presence] of the angels over one sinner that repenteth.'

"[The Pharisees and Sadducees are] so righteous they will be damned. Anyhow, you cannot save them; [it is like] rain off from a goose's back. 'Great I, little you!'

"'A certain man had two sons,' and so forth. '[I] am a poor publican, a sinner.' [He] humbled [himself], spending [his] bread and living. 'I'll return to my father's house, to Jesus.' 'You Pharisees [are] so righteous you cannot be touched.' 'I will arise and claim not [to] be a Pharisee or Sadducee. I claim not to be a son. Do not let me starve.' . . . All that is meant is brought to bear upon the Pharisee, Sadducee, the publican, and sinners. [The] eldest son: Pharisees and Sadducees murmuring and complaining because Jesus sat with publicans and sinners. . . .

"[The] dealing of God with individual men [is] always righteous. [They] always have access to [the] throne of God. . . . Servants of God of the last days, myself and those I have ordained, have the priesthood and a mission—to the publicans and sinners" (Discourse, 29 January 1843, recorded by Willard Richards, as cited in Jackson, *Joseph Smith's Commentary*, 123–24; see also Journal, December 1842–June 1844; Book 1, 21 December 1842–10 March 1843, The Joseph Smith Papers, accessed 21 February 2014, http://josephsmithpapers.org/paperSummary /journal-december-1842-june-1844-book-1-21-december-1842 -10-march-1843?p=168).

Joseph Smith Translation

The disciples may have been wrestling with the high price of giving up everything for the sake of the kingdom of God. The Joseph Smith Translation changes turn Jesus's teachings into a direct response to their concerns: "*Wherefore, settle this in your hearts, that ye will do the things which I shall teach and command you.* For which of you, intending to build a tower, sitteth not down first, and counteth the cost, whether he *has money* to finish *his work?*" (Luke 14:26; italics indicate changes to the KJV text).

When Jesus said, "It is easier for a camel to go through the eye of a needle, than for a rich man to enter into the kingdom of God," His disciples asked, "Who then can be saved?" An important JST addition to Matthew helped the disciples understand how their sacrifice would enable God to bless them: "But Jesus beheld *their thoughts,* and said unto them, With men this is impossible; but *if they will forsake all things for my sake,* with God *whatsoever* things *I speak* are possible" (JST Matthew 19:26; italics indicate changes to the KJV text).

STUDY QUESTIONS

1. Several of Jesus's parables discuss things that are lost. What meaning can we find in that emphasis on lost things?
2. Which of the two sons in the parable of the prodigal son was more wasteful? Were each of the two sons prodigal?
3. Who has been a good neighbor to you? Why do you consider that person a good neighbor? How can you be a better neighbor?

CHAPTER 28

THE LAST WINTER

In John 10, Jesus's attention shifts toward His other sheep: "And other sheep I have, which are not of this fold: them also I must bring, and they shall hear my voice; and there shall be one fold, and one shepherd" (John 10:16). With these momentous words, Jesus openly and plainly declared to all believers that His work would no longer be relegated to a single nation at a single point in time.

Earlier, Jesus had forbidden His disciples to minister to the Samaritans and the Gentiles, but now these restrictions seem to give way to a broader perspective of the salvation of all humankind. The Book of Mormon indicates that Jesus was referring not just to the Gentiles (3 Nephi 15:17, 21; 16:1), and the New Testament verses testify that He loves all His children and seeks to bring all of the faithful into a single fold.

This part of the Gospel of John also includes the account of the raising of Lazarus, a story that is told in great detail and the narration for which is much longer than any of the other miracle stories. Perhaps there is more detail because Lazarus and his sisters were Jesus's close personal friends: "Jesus loved Martha, and her sister, and Lazarus" (John 11:5). Another reason may be that, in John, this episode leads to Jesus's arrest and execution. In the synoptic Gospels, the cleansing of the temple leads to His arrest and execution.

The story at its most basic level is a story of trust: the disciples must trust that their lives will be spared if they travel to Jerusalem (John 11:17), Martha and Mary must trust that Jesus has power to heal their brother (John 11:22, 32), and Jesus trusts that the Father will hear Him and grant His request to raise Lazarus (John 11:41–42).

The story also deals with the fundamental issue of opposition: in healing Lazarus, Jesus fans the flames of opposition against Him. His enemies now seek more openly to kill Him (John 11:47–57). It seems that the report of the raising of Lazarus spread like wildfire, and a group of Jewish leaders convened a council to find a way to put Jesus to death. Their fear was that eventually everyone would believe in Jesus and that Rome would punish them for insubordination.

The raising of Lazarus prefigures Jesus's Resurrection, but Lazarus returned to life in a mortal body and Jesus rose from the tomb in a glorified, resurrected body.

Since 1915

Jesus and Lazarus. According to the Gospel of John, Jesus and Lazarus were friends (John 11:3), and when He mingled with the mourners in Bethany after Lazarus's death, "Jesus wept" (John 11:35). Displays of emotion are rare in Gospel accounts; this was a very personal moment for Jesus and His disciples. John reports that Jesus groaned, or expressed deep emotions, while approaching Lazarus's grave (John 11:38).

This is one of the few stories that directly address the topic of friendship. Jesus was a close friend of Lazarus and his sisters, Mary and Martha. The healing of Lazarus, however, may have started a chain reaction: "But the chief priests consulted that they might put Lazarus also to death; because that by reason of him many of the Jews went away, and believed on Jesus" (John 12:10–11). This story is a literal fulfillment of Jesus's teaching, "Greater love hath no man than this, that a man lay down his life for his friends" (John 15:13). Jesus literally gave His life for having given life to Lazarus.

Caiaphas. Elder Talmage provides a detailed discussion of Joseph Caiaphas, the Jewish high priest at the time of Jesus's ministry (501). The New Testament depicts Caiaphas as Jesus's chief opponent. In 1990, twelve ossuaries (boxes containing bones) were discovered in a burial cave near Jerusalem. One of the beautifully decorated boxes has the words "Joseph, son of Caiaphas" inscribed on it in two places. It contained the bones of a sixty-year-old male generally assumed to be the Joseph Caiaphas mentioned in the New Testament or at least someone belonging to his family.

Joseph Smith Translation

The Joseph Smith Translation changes in Luke 16 are significant: "*And they said unto him, We have the law, and the prophets; but as for this man we will not receive him to be our ruler; for he maketh himself to be a judge over us. Then said Jesus unto them,* The law and the prophets *testify of me; yea, and all the prophets who have written, even* until John, *have foretold of these days.* Since that time, the kingdom of God is preached, and every man *who seeketh truth* presseth into it. And it is easier for heaven and earth to pass, than *for* one tittle of the law to fail" (JST Luke 16:16–17; italics indicate changes to the KJV text).

In the JST, few changes are made to the story of the raising of Lazarus, but one addition provides insight into the disciple Thomas's comment about returning to Bethany: "Then said Thomas, which is called Didymus, unto his fellowdisciples, Let us also go, that we may die with him. *For they feared lest the Jews should take Jesus and put him to death, for as yet they did not understand the power of God"* (JST John 11:16; italics indicate changes to the KJV text). Because an attempt had been made to kill Jesus during a previous visit to the city (John 8:59), the dread of returning to Jerusalem is a thread running through the Gospel of John.

STUDY QUESTIONS

1. When have you recognized Jesus's voice in your life? What can you do to be aware of it more often?
2. What impressed or inspired you as you read about Jesus's raising of Lazarus from the dead?
3. Why did Jesus teach the Jews about His "other sheep"?

CHAPTER 29

ON TO JERUSALEM

To help His followers come to terms with and understand the
need for His sacrificial death, Jesus prophesied about the events
that would occur in Jerusalem during the final week of His mortal
ministry. Sometimes the prophecies are explicit, and sometimes
they are veiled.

A powerful prophecy of His impending suffering and death
was given one week before the experiences that took place on
the Mount of Transfiguration. Matthew relates: "From that time
forth began Jesus to shew unto his disciples, how that he must go
unto Jerusalem, and suffer many things of the elders and chief
priests and scribes, and be killed, and be raised again the third
day" (Matthew 16:21).

Shortly before His triumphal entry into Jerusalem, Jesus
taught plainly for the third time, "Behold, we go up to Jerusalem;
and the Son of man shall be betrayed unto the chief priests and
unto the scribes, and they shall condemn him to death, and

shall deliver him to the Gentiles to mock, and to scourge, and to crucify him: and the third day he shall rise again" (Matthew 20:18–19).

The triumphal entry is the most significant event in this chapter of *Jesus the Christ* and was another provocation of Jesus's enemies. Jesus procured a donkey and rode through the Kidron Valley on the east side of Jerusalem and up through the eastern gate of the Jerusalem temple. The Jewish leaders were scandalized by what they considered to be an imposter's enactment of the Old Testament prophecy about the messianic king entering the Holy City (Zechariah 9) or a re-creation of Solomon's coronation (1 Kings 1:33–40).

For Jesus's followers, it was a moment of triumphal declaration that He had come to Jerusalem in power. Chanting a messianic psalm, "Hosanna to the Son of David: Blessed is he that cometh in the name of the Lord; Hosanna in the highest" (Matthew 21:9; cf. Psalms 118:26), they expressed their conviction that Jesus was the Davidic Messiah and welcomed Him into His house (the temple). Whether Jesus encouraged their actions we cannot tell, but no Gospel reports Him doing anything to silence their praise and singing.

The full impact of the triumphal entry cannot be understood apart from Jesus's act of cleansing the temple (see chapter 30). Had the triumphal entry stopped short of the cleansing of the temple, Jesus's life might have been spared and His enemies might have found no reason to have Him arrested and taken before Pilate.

In this chapter, Elder Talmage also discusses a gathering in Bethany of Jesus and several of His close friends—Mary, Martha, and Lazarus. Matthew informs us that they were dining at the house of Simon the leper (Matthew 26:6), who may have been healed by Jesus. Elder Talmage discusses the possible relationships among Simon, Lazarus, Mary, and Martha (522–23).

While they were dining together, Mary took a small jar or bottle of incense and used it to anoint Jesus's head and feet. She then dried His feet with her hair (John 12:3).

It was customary for first-century hosts to provide a basin of water and a towel with which visitors could wash their feet when they arrived. In the homes of the wealthy, a servant or slave might assist with the washing. Mary's anointing, or washing, of Jesus's feet after the group had reclined for dinner would have been highly unusual and would have drawn a great deal of notice because she singled out Jesus, washed and dried His feet much later after their arrival, and performed the action herself. Obviously, there must have been a connection between the recent raising of Lazarus, Mary's brother, and the deep devotion and respect she showed to Jesus on this occasion. When questions arose about whether her actions were appropriate, Jesus took the opportunity to once again foretell His imminent death: "For in that she hath poured this ointment on my body, she did it for my burial" (Matthew 26:12). He also foretold that this loving act of Mary's would be known wherever the gospel would be "preached in the whole world . . . for a memorial of her" (Matthew 26:13).

Since 1915

The Passion Week. The term "Passion Week," sometimes referred to as "Holy Week," is used to describe the last week of Jesus's mortal life. It is a week of central significance in all four Gospel accounts and includes all the events that comprise the Atonement. The idea of Passion Week derives from the Latin word *passio,* meaning "suffering," because it is the time when Jesus suffered for humankind. The term *passion* is ancient and was used by Luke (Greek, *pathio*) to refer to the death of Jesus: "To whom also he shewed himself alive after his *passion* by many infallible proofs, being seen of them forty days, and speaking of the things pertaining to the kingdom of God" (Acts 1:3; emphasis added). The four passion narratives represent the earliest Christian attempts to make sense of Jesus's death.

Three hundred pence. Elder Talmage provides the 1915 monetary equivalent for the costly ointment used by Mary to anoint Jesus's head and feet as "forty-five dollars" (512). That amount would be close to $150 today.

Son of Man. Jesus refers to Himself as the "Son of Man" some eighty-two times in the Gospels. A term filled with meaning, it became an important messianic image for some first-century Jews. First, it may refer to "the Son of man" mentioned in Daniel—an agent of God who descends in the clouds to judge the wicked and vindicate the righteous (Daniel 7:13–14). Second, as Elder Talmage suggests, the term may refer to the truth revealed in Moses 6: "Man of Holiness is his name, and the name of his Only Begotten is the Son of Man, even Jesus Christ, a righteous Judge, who shall come in the meridian of time" (Moses 6:57). These positions are not exclusive of each other. In examining each reference to "Son of man," we may discover that Jesus used "Son of man" in both contexts. When Jesus spoke to His Apostles about the death of the Son of Man, they may have recalled His asking them a few weeks earlier, "Whom do men say that I the Son of man am?" (Matthew 16:13).

Day of the triumphal entry. Jesus "came to Bethany" "six days before the Passover" (John 12:1). The triumphal entry took place the next day (John 12:12). According to the Jewish manner of reckoning, the beginning of Passover occurred at sundown on Friday evening, and because it was late March or early April, sundown occurred between 6:30 and 7:00 P.M. Thus, if we count back six inclusive days from Friday evening, the triumphal entry occurred on Sunday. The date is important because it defines the beginning of the Passion Week. Elder Talmage notes that today "the Sunday before Easter is annually celebrated by many Christian sects as Palm Sunday, in commemoration of our Lord's triumphal entry into Jerusalem" (517).

JOSEPH SMITH TRANSLATION

Four accounts of the anointing of Jesus are given in the Gospels. In the synoptic Gospels (Matthew, Mark, and Luke), the woman is unnamed. In John, she is identified as Mary of Bethany, the sister of Martha and Lazarus. The Joseph Smith Translation helps to connect the accounts:

"And *Jesus* being in Bethany in the house of Simon the leper, as he sat at meat, there came a woman having an alabaster box of ointment of spikenard very precious; and she brake the box, and poured *the ointment* on his head. There were *among the disciples who* had indignation. . . . And Jesus said *unto them,* Let her alone; why trouble ye her? *For* she hath wrought a good work on me. . . . She *has* done what she could, *and this which she has done unto me shall be had in remembrance in generations to come, wherever my gospel shall be preached; for verily* she *has* come *beforehand* to anoint my body to the burying" (JST Mark 14:3–4, 6, 8; italics indicate changes to the KJV text).

STUDY QUESTIONS

1. At various times during Jesus's ministry, He taught of His own impending death and Resurrection. Why did He reveal to His disciples the events of His final week in Jerusalem?

2. Why were the disciples slow to understand Jesus's words about His departure?

3. Think of a time when you were slow to understand the Lord's will. Why do you think this was the case? What have you learned from this chapter that will help you avoid being "slow to understand" the Lord's will again?

CHAPTER 30

JESUS RETURNS TO
THE TEMPLE DAILY

This chapter opens with a unique miracle—the cursing of the fig tree. Jesus's actions usually blessed and healed, but in this instance, the action of cursing demonstrated His power to pronounce judgment. Commentators have struggled to arrive at a consensus on the complete meaning of the event, but a lesson may be drawn from Elder Talmage's insight: Church activity without the accompanying fruits of repentance and renewal will not save us.

Elder Talmage now focuses his attention on the cleansing of the temple (Matthew 21:12–13; cf. Talmage, 527–30). This act was integrally connected to the triumphal entry, as discussed in chapter 29. The sequence of the two events laid the foundation for the arrest and condemnation of the Lord.

Fundamentally, the triumphal entry and the subsequent cleansing of the temple were attacks on the chief priests' power and authority at the temple. The custom of the day required pilgrims who entered the temple complex to exchange their currency, which often were imprinted with pagan images, for the official temple currency that was then used to purchase animals and birds for sacrifice. Those who wished to offer an animal sacrifice were required to have that animal confirmed in order to meet the strict requirements of the law of Moses.

To facilitate these requirements, the chief priests set up booths outside the temple. The practice was not out of line with the Mosaic instructions; however, some later sources suggest that the chief priests inflated prices in fees both for exchanging money and for sacrificial animals. Jesus's actions, then, would have been directed at corrupt temple authorities who made profits on otherwise understandable and useful transactions.

Scholars believe that the practice of selling sacrificial animals took place in the Court of the Gentiles near the south side of the temple and not in the temple proper.

The Gospel accounts clearly indicate that, upon entering the temple, Jesus found some pieces of rope or other cord-like material and fashioned a small whip that He used to drive the sacrificial animals out of the temple courtyard. He then overturned the tables of the moneychangers. The crowd who had been singing praises to Him may have looked favorably upon these actions, but His enemies saw them as a direct attack upon their privileges and authority.

Additionally, Rome and Roman governors had an extremely low tolerance for public disturbances. As a result, Jesus's involvement in these events at the temple would have garnered the attention of the local authorities and could have resulted in arrest and punishment, even possible death, for Jesus and some of His followers. Perhaps His enemies were not powerful enough to convince the Roman authorities to take action against Him. Perhaps the people's support of Him was too overwhelming at this point, or perhaps Jesus simply departed before the authorities had time to apprehend Him (Matthew 21:12–17).

SINCE 1915

The cleansing of the temple. Under normal circumstances in a Roman imperial province, Jesus's cleansing of the temple would have elicited a fairly swift and decisive response. Punishments might have ranged from beating, scourging, and imprisonment to crucifixion. Jesus's actions and teachings relating to the temple became the central issue in His trial, when witnesses reported that "this fellow said, I am able to destroy the temple of God, and to build it in three days" (Matthew 26:61). This, combined with the recent temple cleansing, painted a negative portrait of His intentions. In the synoptic Gospels, this action at the beginning of Passion Week led to Jesus's death at week's end.

JOSEPH SMITH'S TEACHINGS

Luke 22:1–14. "In the 22nd chapter of Luke's account of the Messiah, we find the kingdom of heaven likened unto a king who made a marriage for his son. That his son was the Messiah will not be disputed, since it was the *kingdom of heaven* that was represented in the parable; and that the saints, or those who are found faithful to the Lord, are the individuals who will be found worthy to inherit a seat at the marriage supper is evident from the sayings of John in Revelation: 'the marriage of the Lamb is come, and his wife hath made herself ready. And to her was granted that she should be arrayed in fine linen, clean and white: for the fine linen is the righteousness of saints' (Revelation 19:7–8)" ("The Elders of the Church in Kirtland, to Their Brethren Abroad," *Evening and Morning Star,* March 1834, 144).

Matthew 22:14. "There has been a great difficulty in getting anything into the heads of this generation. . . . Even the Saints are slow to understand. I have tried for a number of years to get the minds of the Saints prepared to receive the things of God, but we frequently see [that] some of them, after suffering all they have for the work of God, will fly to pieces like glass as soon as anything comes that is contrary to their traditions. They cannot stand the fire at all. How many will be able to abide a celestial law and go through and receive their exaltation? I am unable to say, but many are called, and few are chosen" (Discourse, 21 January 1844, recorded by Wilford Woodruff, as cited in Jackson, *Joseph Smith's Commentary,* 102).

JOSEPH SMITH TRANSLATION

One of the parables that Jesus delivered shortly after His triumphal entry into Jerusalem was the parable of the wicked husbandman. The Joseph Smith Translation refocuses the intent of this parable and sharpens its directness: "For John came unto you in the way of righteousness *and bore record of me,* and ye believed him not: but the publicans and the harlots believed him: and ye, *afterwards,* when ye had seen *me* repented not, that ye might believe him*; for he that believed not John concerning me, cannot believe me, except he first repent; and except ye repent, the preaching of John shall condemn you in that day of judgment. And again,* hear another parable: *for unto you that believe not, I speak in parables, that your unrighteousness may be rewarded unto you. Behold* there was a certain householder, *who* planted a vineyard, and hedged it round about, and digged a winepress in it, and built a tower, and let it out to husbandmen, and went into a far country" (JST Matthew 21:32–33; italics indicate changes to the KJV text).

STUDY QUESTIONS

1. What are the fruits of gospel living? (2 Peter 1:1–8; Galatians
    5:22–26; and James 2:14–20).

2. How do we ensure that we not only attend church or the
    temple but also bear fruit, instead of being like the barren fig
    tree?

3. When Jesus was confronted by the Jewish elders regarding
    His cleansing the temple, He responded by teaching in par-
    ables. Matthew includes Jesus's teaching on why He used par-
    ables (Matthew 13:10–17). How does the information from
    Matthew help you understand Jesus's intent in teaching in
    parables following His triumphal entry?

CHAPTER 31

THE CLOSE OF OUR
LORD'S PUBLIC MINISTRY

This chapter of *Jesus the Christ* reviews a conspiracy to kill Jesus, a question about the Resurrection, the "great commandment," the problem of religious hypocrisy, Jesus's final withdrawal from the temple, and a prophecy about its destruction. Additionally, Elder Talmage relates a touching story about a widow's offering at the temple.

As He had earlier in His ministry, Jesus sat pondering in the temple courtyard. He noticed a number of people giving donations to the temple treasury. According to the evangelists (Mark 12:41), He observed the wealthy giving large amounts of money, and then "there came a certain poor widow, and she threw in two mites, which make a farthing. And he called unto him his disciples, and saith unto them, Verily I say unto you, That this poor widow hath cast more in, than all they which have cast into the treasury" (Mark 12:42–43).

We do not know the precise value of the two lepta (mites) the woman gave to the temple treasury, but two of them combined were probably much less than the value of a Roman denarius. Scholars have commonly reported that in New Testament times, a denarius was approximately the payment for a day's wage (see Matthew 20:1–17, where a denarius is translated as "penny"). Recently discovered pay receipts from the first century have shown, however, that an individual workman could receive up to eight denarii for a regular day of physical labor. Thus, the woman's two mites may have equaled the wage an able-bodied male workman would receive for about a half hour of labor in good circumstances.

Matthew 22 gathers together a number of similar events, placing them side by side in a single chapter. These events, however, may have happened over a series of a few days or over the whole course of Jesus's mortal ministry. Matthew may have included them all together because they revolve around questions, some asked with ill intent and others for purposes of clarification.

After delivering the parable of the marriage of the king's son, Jesus was asked whether He considered it lawful to pay taxes to Rome. The Jewish leaders asked this question as a thinly disguised attempt to generate a complaint against Jesus. Instead of offering a direct answer, Jesus gave them some true perspective on the issue. First, he asked to see the tribute money and was shown a coin. He asked, "Whose is this image?" His questioners replied, "Caesar's." Then, "saith he unto them, Render therefore unto Caesar the things which are Caesar's; and unto God the things that are God's" (Matthew 22:21).

Some today may seek to use Jesus's words to support their own political agenda, but He was not espousing any philosophy regarding government and taxation. He may, however, have been implying the obvious irony that all things belong to God.

A similar situation occurred when the Sadducees asked Jesus a question about the resurrection (Matthew 22:23–33). The best historical sources indicate that the Sadducees likely did not believe in the resurrection, and they presented a riddle to disprove the reality of a physical resurrection. We should expect, then, that Jesus would perceive their intended purpose. They asked which brother a woman, who had married seven brothers, would be given to in the resurrection.

Rather than answer their question, Jesus answered their intent: "Ye do err, not knowing the scriptures, nor the power of God. For in the resurrection they neither marry, nor are given in marriage, but are as the angels of God in heaven" (Matthew 22:29–30).

There are several ways to interpret Jesus's answer, but because His response took recourse in the scriptures, we conclude that the answer is in the scriptures. Further, Jesus alludes to the doctrine taught in Restoration scripture that mortality is the time for marriage according to God's law and that God will decide what happens in the next life (Doctrine and Covenants 131:1–4; 132:16). Many things are left unsaid in His answer, and those desiring revelation about the eternal nature of marriage or humankind's role in the hereafter should seek the scriptures on the topic—not a response given to an antagonistic question.

In one of His final public statements, Jesus openly denounced the priests and Pharisees for their small-minded pettiness. In fact, an entire chapter is devoted to the subject (Matthew 23). Its tone is unlike anything else in the Gospels and extends well beyond any previous denunciations that Jesus gave.

SINCE 1915

Zacharias. An editorial in the Church's Nauvoo newspaper, *Times and Seasons,* likely written by W. W. Phelps or John Taylor, states: "Let us come into New Testament times—so many are ever praising the Lord and his apostles. We will commence with John the Baptist. When Herod's edict went forth to destroy the young children, John was about six months older than Jesus, and came under this hellish edict, and Zachariah caused his mother to take him into the mountains, where he was raised on locusts and wild honey. When his father refused to discover his hiding place, and being the officiating high priest at the Temple that year, was slain by Herod's order, between the porch and the altar, as Jesus said" ("Persecution of the Prophets," *Times and Seasons,* 1 September 1842, 902).

This reference to the slaying of Zacharias is found in Matthew 23:35, which reads, "That upon you may come all the righteous blood shed upon the earth, from the blood of righteous Abel unto the blood of Zacharias son of Barachias, whom ye slew between the temple and the altar." Today, however, scholars believe that the person named Zacharias in this verse was not the father of John the Baptist but the Old Testament prophet Zechariah (Zechariah 1:1 refers to him as Zechariah son of Berechiah) or Zechariah son of Jehoiada (2 Chronicles 24:20).

Joseph Smith, W. W. Phelps, and John Taylor had acquired a copy of William Hone's influential translation of the Christian apocrypha in 1842. In that collection was a text that is now referred to as the *Infancy Gospel of James* (*Protoevangelium of James*). In that work, the third-century anonymous author mistakenly connects Zacharias, the father of John the Baptist, with the Zacharias in Matthew 23:35, and we are now confident that the incorrect statement in the editorial in the *Times and Seasons* is based on the *Infancy Gospel of James.*

Jesus's statement in Matthew 23:35 was intended to declare that those who opposed Jesus would share in the responsibility for the deaths of Old Testament martyrs, beginning with the first, Abel, and extending to the last martyr of the Old Testament—Zacharias son of Barachias.

Strain at a gnat, and swallow a camel. This passage from the King James Version is mistranslated and ought to read "strain out a gnat, and swallow a camel" (557, where Elder Talmage cites the Revised Version). At issue was the practice of straining drinks to make sure the liquid was pure in a religious sense. Because gnats were considered unclean in the law of Moses, straining liquid before drinking ensured a person would not ingest even a tiny gnat. Jesus drew attention to the great care that the Jews took to avoid swallowing a tiny gnat while metaphorically swallowing a whole camel, also considered unclean in the law of Moses. In other words, they scrupulously worried about the small details of the law but condoned large infractions, such as abuse of temple funds, participation in Roman power politics, and the adoption of aristocratic lifestyles at the expense of the poor.

JOSEPH SMITH'S TEACHINGS

Matthew 23:37–38. "What was the object of gathering the Jews together, or the people of God in any age of the world? The main object was to build unto the Lord a house, whereby he could reveal unto his people the ordinances of his house and the glories of his kingdom, and teach the people the ways of salvation. For there are certain ordinances and principles that when they are taught and practiced must be done in a place or house built for that purpose. This was purposed in the mind of God before the world was, and it was for this purpose that God designed to gather together the Jews oft. But they would not. It is for the same purpose that God gathers together the people in the last days, to build unto the Lord a house to prepare them for the ordinances, endowment, washings, and anointings. . . . It was one reason why Jesus said, 'How oft would I have gathered you (the Jews) together'" (Discourse, 11 June 1843, recorded by Wilford Woodruff, as cited in Jackson, *Joseph Smith's Commentary,* 104).

JOSEPH SMITH TRANSLATION

A colorful expression in Jesus's denunciation of hypocritical religious leaders has become a well-known aphorism: "strain at a gnat, and swallow a camel." The Joseph Smith Translation adds more information to this verse: "*You* blind guides, *who* strain at a gnat, and swallow a camel; *who make yourselves appear unto men that ye would not commit the least sin, and yet ye yourselves, transgress the whole law*" (JST Matthew 23:24; italics indicate changes to the KJV text).

STUDY QUESTIONS

1. What does Jesus's discussion regarding what the people owe Caesar and what they owe God mean in a modern setting?
2. What can you do to live the two great commandments more fully this week?
3. What is hypocrisy? Why does the Lord condemn it so strongly? What is the difference between someone whose actions and life fall short of perfect obedience (a fallible disciple) and someone who "plays a part"?
4. In what ways do you *act* in your religious life instead of *living* it? What can you do to avoid hypocrisy this week? This month? This year?

CHAPTER 32

FURTHER INSTRUCTION
TO THE APOSTLES

Near the middle of the Passion Week, on Wednesday or perhaps even Thursday morning, Jesus delivered a discourse to His disciples while they were gathered together on the Mount of Olives. The Mount of Olives is not far from the Jerusalem temple, and indeed Jesus and His disciples could see the temple while standing on the Mount of Olives. In this setting, Jesus gathered together His disciples and taught them about His return and the calamities that would follow His death. Today, we refer to that discourse as the Olivet discourse because of where it took place.

The New Testament contains three versions of the same sermon: Matthew 24, Mark 13, and Luke 21:5–38; a revised version of the sermon is found in the Joseph Smith Translation of the Bible (Joseph Smith–Matthew; see also JST Mark 13). Matthew is the most explicit about the discourse being delivered to the disciples: "And Jesus went out, and departed from the temple: and his disciples came to him for to shew him the buildings of the temple" (Matthew 24:1). Using the Jerusalem temple as a back-drop, Jesus discussed the future of the temple as well as the fate of the city of Jerusalem.

The discourse touches upon two main time periods: (1) events that would occur almost immediately and that would involve Jesus's disciples and (2) future events that would take place prior to the Lord's return in glory. This information is not evident from the structure of the sermon as contained in the New Testament accounts, but it is evident in Joseph Smith–Matthew, which retains much of the original wording of Matthew's account but also gives his account a slightly altered structure.

"And as he sat upon the Mount of Olives, the disciples came unto him privately, saying: Tell us when shall these things be which thou hast said concerning the destruction of the temple, and the Jews; and what is the sign of thy coming, and of the end of the world, or the destruction of the wicked, which is the end of the world?" (Joseph Smith–Matthew 1:4). The questions of the disciples explicitly refer to two different time periods, the time of the destruction of the temple that occurred in AD 70 and events occurring at "the end of the world."

Following the original context of the sermon, Jesus's disciples sought Him out to ask Him a question regarding some things He had taught them. He had recently been explicit in saying that He would soon die and be resurrected, and the disciples came to Him for clarification. Additionally in the sermon, Jesus taught principles of preparedness rather than predictions of what to prepare for. He told His disciples to remember the days of Noah (Matthew 24:38) and to remember that even the "goodman of the house" would be caught off guard (Matthew 24:43). What emerges from this sermon is the idea that Jesus had foreseen the calamities that would occur and that, in His foreseeing and foretelling them, the disciples would shortly know that Jesus had not miscalculated the cost of their discipleship. He was aware of what they would experience.

Similar to Matthew 13, where seven parables are gathered into a single chapter, Matthew 25 gathers some of Jesus's parables that are thematically linked. The three parables—the parable of the ten virgins, the parable of the talents, and the parable of the sheep and goats—deal with preparation and have been classified by scholars as parables of preparation. They warn the disciples to prepare for the Lord's Second Coming. Additionally, they all deal collectively with what it means to sin. Obviously, this was a question of great importance for the early Church, which would soon leave behind the law of Moses and its precise definitions of sin.

For those seeking to be obedient in the dispensations when God asks them to follow the Holy Spirit, the question of what defines sin will always be prevalent. In Matthew 25, Jesus addresses the topic directly by focusing on some interesting points. In the three parables, all those who are condemned or chastised receive condemnation or chastisement because of what they failed to do (omission) rather than for what they did wrong (commission). In the parable of the ten virgins, for example, the five unwise virgins were all invited guests. They were in the right place at the right time with the right supplies. But in the end, they were negligent in knowing how much oil to bring with them. Similarly, the unwise person in the parable of the talents failed to increase the amount of money he was given, even though he was able to return the original investment unharmed. The disciples learned the powerful lesson that God looks also at what we fail to do, not only at what we do wrong.

SINCE 1915

Joseph Smith–Matthew. Over the course of his lifetime, Joseph Smith "translated" the entire Bible. Although not a translation in the traditional sense, which generally means translating from one language into a new language, this work is best understood as an "inspired translation." He did not have any ancient Greek manuscripts but instead worked from an English Bible, an 1828 edition of the King James Version printed by H. & E. Phinney.

Joseph Smith's translation from Matthew was published in 1842 as "Extracts from the New Translation" in *Times and Seasons*. Later it was reprinted in the Pearl of Great Price and published in England in 1851 under the title "An Extract from a Translation of the Bible," which is the inspired translation of Matthew 23:39–24:51.

JOSEPH SMITH'S TEACHINGS

Matthew 24:6–13 (Joseph Smith–Matthew 1:28–30). "It is a false idea that the Saints will escape all the judgments while the wicked suffer, for all flesh is subject to suffer, and the righteous shall hardly escape. Still, many of the Saints will escape, for the just shall live by faith. Yet many of the righteous shall fall prey to disease, to pestilence, and so forth, by reason of the weakness of the flesh, and yet be saved in the kingdom of God" (Discourse, 29 September 1839, recorded by James Mulholland, as cited in Jackson, *Joseph Smith's Commentary*, 105; see also Ehat and Cook, *Words of Joseph Smith*, 15).

JOSEPH SMITH TRANSLATION

Changes in Matthew 21 show why Jesus spoke in parables to the crowds. The changes demonstrate that the method of teaching in parables was effective for its intended purpose: "*And again,* hear another parable: *for unto you that believe not, I speak in parables, that your unrighteousness may be rewarded unto you*" (JST Matthew 21:33; italics indicate changes to the KJV text). These changes reflect a similar statement the Lord gave in Matthew 13:10–17.

In the same chapter is found a change that is related to how we understand the parables, but in this change the disciples come to understand Jesus's future more fully, perhaps in part because they were beginning to understand His intentions in speaking in parables and His reasons for condemning the Pharisees: "For I say unto you, *that you* shall not see me henceforth, *and know that I am he of whom it is written by the prophets, until you* shall say, Blessed is he *who* cometh in the name of the Lord, *in the clouds of heaven, and all the holy angels with him. Then understood his disciples that he should come again on the earth, after that he was glorified and crowned on the right hand of God*" (JST Matthew 23:39; italics indicate changes to the KJV text).

The most substantial change made to a verse in these chapters is also the result of an explanation of a parable—this one a short parable on the eagles and the carcass. The verse is also in Joseph Smith–Matthew 1:27, but the fuller explanation is given only in Luke in the Joseph Smith Translation and is not included in the Matthew changes. The verse in JST Luke reads: "And they answered and said unto him, Where, Lord, *shall they be taken?* And he said unto them, Wheresoever the body is *gathered; or, in other words, whithersoever the saints are gathered,* thither will the eagles be gathered together, *or thither will the remainder be gathered together. This he spake signifying the gathering of his saints; and of angels descending and gathering the remainder unto them; the one from the bed, the other from the grinding, and the other from the field, whithersoever he listeth. For verily there shall be new heavens and a new earth, wherein dwelleth righteousness. And there shall be no unclean thing; for the earth becoming old, even as a garment, having waxed in corruption, wherefore it vanisheth away, and the footstool remaineth sanctified, cleansed from all sin*" (JST Luke 17:37; italics indicate changes to the KJV text).

Study Questions

1. What important changes to the Olivet discourse did the Lord give to the Prophet Joseph Smith?
2. How do you feel when you have not prepared in ways similar to the foolish virgins? How do you feel when you are more like the wise virgins?
3. Why does Jesus continue to tell His disciples about His betrayal and death?

CHAPTER 33

THE LAST SUPPER
AND THE BETRAYAL

The synoptic Gospels highlight Jesus's Last Supper on Thursday evening as a Passover meal (Seder) because it represented the establishment of a new covenant when Jesus took the symbols of the old covenant and invested them with new meaning in light of His approaching death and Resurrection. John indicates that the Last Supper occurred the day before Passover because Jesus died at the very moment the Passover lambs were being sacrificed in the temple.

Whether the Last Supper was a Passover meal or not, we know that Jesus met with His disciples on Thursday evening before He was crucified. While at dinner, Jesus took the opportunity to teach His disciples and to prepare them for His departure. He also informed them that one among the Twelve would betray Him. The Greek word translated as *betray* in the Gospels does not have the same weight as the English word *betray* and means something more akin to "deliver something to someone" or "handing over."

At some point, Judas Iscariot arose from the supper and departed into the night to do what he had planned to do. John records that after Judas had departed, Jesus took a towel and a basin of water and started to wash the feet of the disciples (John 13:4–5). As noted earlier, guests could expect a basin of water and a towel so they could wash their own feet when they arrived at someone's home. Washing of feet was generally done upon a guest's entering the house. In homes of the wealthy, a servant (slave) might have assisted.

In this story, Jesus washes the disciples' feet after dinner, not as they enter the room to begin the dinner. Additionally, Jesus's actions are characteristic of what a servant did, and the contrast is striking—the Lord of all became the servant of all. After Peter understood what was happening, he declared, "Lord, not my feet only, but also my hands and my head" (John 13:9). Ultimately, Jesus washed the feet of the eleven remaining disciples, and then sometime thereafter He sang a hymn with them and departed (Matthew 26:30).

The material covered in John 13–17, which is unique to John's account, details some of Jesus's most profound teachings, the contents of which were reserved for a select group of disciples and followers on the eve of Jesus's crucifixion. From the tone of the discourse given after Jesus washed the disciples' feet, He clearly was aware of His impending death and the sequence of events that were to befall Him.

Jesus began the discourse by revealing to His disciples His one new commandment, the one that defined what He expected of them: "A new commandment I give unto you, That ye love one another; as I have loved you, that ye also love one another. By this shall all men know that ye are my disciples, if ye have love one to another" (John 13:34–35).

Love is the basis of the law of Moses, and no one could have been surprised that Jesus taught about love. What was new in this commandment is that Jesus asked His disciples to "love one another; as I have loved you." Those often-quoted words not only formed the foundation for everything else that would be said that evening but also described in principle everything that Jesus was about to do.

In John 15–16, Jesus discusses how a relationship based on love defines our relationship with God and His Son. Love is the defining characteristic of discipleship, and He reminds the disciples that even though their relationship with God will thrive if they continue to love Him, they will eventually be persecuted for that relationship. In these two chapters, the disciples gain their first open view of what is meant by suffering with Christ and suffering like Christ.

John 17 is formally a prayer that is today referred to as the great Intercessory Prayer or the great High Priestly Prayer because in the prayer, Jesus acts as the high priest of Israel who makes intercession for all humankind. The Gospel of John makes no mention of a prayer in Gethsemane, and it may be that the longer prayer in John 17 partially represents the prayer in Gethsemane.

The prayer is powerful for its details and images of preparing the disciples, who will lead after Jesus's departure. The purpose of the prayer is stated clearly in the opening lines: "And this is life eternal, that they might know thee the only true God, and Jesus Christ, whom thou hast sent" (John 17:3). With the object of obtaining eternal life in sight, we can assume that the prayer was for all of Jesus's followers: "While I was with them in the world, I kept them in thy name: those that thou gavest me I have kept, and none of them is lost, but the son of perdition" (John 17:12).

In the words of the prayer, we see how deeply Jesus cares for

His followers and how He prays for their success: "And the glory which thou gavest me I have given them; that they may be one, even as we are one" (John 17:22).

After the prayer of John 17, Jesus departed from the room where the Last Supper was eaten and traveled with His disciples to a garden on the Mount of Olives. Even though Jesus had been in the city only a few times during His mortal ministry, He apparently had become familiar with the area: "And Judas also, which betrayed him, knew the place: for Jesus ofttimes resorted thither with his disciples" (John 18:2). The location of the garden is not known precisely, but it was across the Kidron Valley on the Mount of Olives, where they could see the temple across the way.

After encouraging His disciples to watch with Him, Jesus ventured farther into the garden and prayed alone. That prayer represents the true beginning of the Atonement, and in it Jesus was almost immediately overwhelmed by a sense of burden: "Then saith he unto them, My soul is exceeding sorrowful, even unto death: tarry ye here, and watch with me. And he went a little further, and fell on his face, and prayed, saying, O my Father, if it be possible, let this cup pass from me: nevertheless not as I will, but as thou wilt" (Matthew 26:38–39).

We cannot know from the available sources all of what occurred in that garden, but the weight of human sin and disorder bore down on Jesus so that "being in an agony he prayed more earnestly: and his sweat was as it were great drops of blood falling down to the ground" (Luke 22:44). We may want to visualize a person being crushed by an immense weight. Reflecting almost two thousand years later on His suffering, Jesus said, "Which suffering caused myself, even God, the greatest of all, to tremble because of pain, and to bleed at every pore, and to suffer both body and spirit—and would that I might not drink the bitter cup, and shrink" (Doctrine and Covenants 19:18).

We are not certain whether Jesus was in the garden for hours or minutes. But we do know that sufficient time had passed for Judas to betray Jesus and for officers from the chief priests and Pharisees to have gathered together a band of soldiers and led them to the garden, where Judas anticipated Jesus would be.

We do not know whether the Apostle John had considered the question of Judas's actions more carefully than the others had or whether he was more aware of what took place that evening. We do learn from John's account that the arresting party did not have direct knowledge of who Jesus was. When they approached Jesus and spoke to Him face to face, they were unaware that they were speaking to Jesus: "Whom seek ye? And they said, Jesus of Nazareth" (John 18:7). If Judas's betrayal were to be defined as a single act, it would be that he revealed the whereabouts of Jesus when He was alone and away from the believing crowds, thus enabling His enemies to arrest Him without incident.

SINCE 1915

Thirty pieces of silver. Elder Talmage describes the 1915 monetary equivalent for the thirty pieces of silver Judas received from the chief priest to hand Jesus over as "approximately seventy dollars" (592). Today that amount equals about four hundred dollars; however, the buying power of the thirty pieces of silver is estimated to be considerably more.

The day of the Last Supper. The synoptic Gospels indicate that the Last Supper was a Passover meal (Matthew 26:17; Mark 14:1–2; Luke 22:1–15) and that the meal took place on the evening prior to the Crucifixion, on Nisan 15 (March-April) (Thursday evening through Friday evening). They depict Jesus finishing supper; going into a garden, where He prayed; and being arrested—all taking place in the evening.

The Gospel of John, however, indicates that the feast of the Passover began at sundown on the evening of the Crucifixion. Thus, the Last Supper would have been eaten on Nisan 14, and the Crucifixion would have taken place on Nisan 15. We note that the discrepancy is not about the days of the week on which these events occurred but rather about the dates of their occurrence.

The Gospel of John also seems aware of another issue of dating: "The Jews therefore, because it was the preparation, that the bodies should not remain upon the cross on the Sabbath day, (for that Sabbath day was an high day,) besought Pilate that their legs might be broken, and that they might be taken away" (John 19:31). The idea that the Sabbath was a "high day" has caused some confusion, but the solution is probably quite simple.

The first day of the Passover was considered a special day, and the Sabbath was considered a holy day. In most years, the first day of the Passover does not fall on a Sabbath; but in the year that Jesus was crucified, the first day of Passover (Nisan 15) may have fallen on the Sabbath, which began on Friday evening. Thus, John's dating of the event to Nisan 14 is probably more correct than the dating in the synoptic Gospels. His awareness that Friday evening was both the Sabbath and the beginning of Passover is more detailed than we find in the synoptic accounts, and that might explain why some families chose to eat the Passover meal on Thursday.

"For this is my blood of the new testament." These words come from Matthew 26:28 and were spoken by Jesus on the night of the Last Supper (see also Mark 14:24; Luke 22:20; 1 Corinthians 11:25). When Jesus spoke these words, He had in His hand the cup of the sacrament, and when He said, "This is my blood of the new testament," He was referring to a new covenant mentioned in the Old Testament (Jeremiah 31:31). The word translated as *testament* is better translated as *covenant* (597, where Elder Talmage cites the Revised Version). Jesus clearly indicated to His disciples that He was extending to them a new covenant in His blood: the sacrament. He was renewing the meaning of the symbols of the old covenant.

Joseph Smith's Teachings

Luke 22:3–4. "From apostates the faithful have received the severest persecutions. Judas was rebuked and immediately betrayed his Lord into the hands of his enemies, because Satan entered into him. There is a supreme intelligence bestowed upon such as obey the gospel with full purpose of heart, which, if sinned against, the apostate is left naked and destitute of the Spirit of God, and they are in truth, nigh unto cursing, and their end is to be burned. When once that light which was in them is taken from them, they become as much darkened as they were previously enlightened. And then, no marvel, if all their power should be enlisted against the truth, and they, Judas-like, seek the destruction of those who were their greatest benefactors! What nearer friend on earth, or in heaven, had Judas than the Savior? And his first object was to destroy him!" ("The Elders of the Church in Kirtland, to Their Brethren Abroad," *Evening and Morning Star,* April 1834, 152).

John 14:16–26. "There are two Comforters spoken of. One is the Holy Ghost, the same as given on the day of Pentecost and that all Saints receive after faith, repentance, and baptism. This first Comforter, or Holy Ghost, has no other effect than pure intelligence. . . . Now what is this other Comforter? It is no more or less than the Lord Jesus Christ himself, and this is the sum and substance of the whole matter, that when any man obtains this last Comforter he will have the personage of Jesus Christ to attend him or appear unto him from time to time, and even he will manifest the Father unto him, and they will take up their abode with him" (The Joseph Smith Papers, accessed 7 July 2014, http://josephsmithpapers.org/paperSummary/history-1838-1856 -volume-c-1-2-november-1838-31-july-1842?p=543).

JOSEPH SMITH TRANSLATION

A change in a passage covered in this chapter offers a timely reminder of how the life of Jesus was not only salvific but also exemplary. His life, which Christians have sought to emulate for centuries, has always been closely studied and commented upon. The Joseph Smith Translation adds a sentence in Matthew that directly commands us to live a life like His: "*And I give unto you a commandment, that ye shall observe to do the things which ye have seen me do, and bear record of me even unto the end.* But I say unto you, I will not drink henceforth of this fruit of the vine, until that day when I drink it new with you in my Father's kingdom" (JST Matthew 26:29; italics indicate changes to the KJV text).

In a change to John 13:10, the JST offers an addition to the practice of washing of the feet as performed by Jesus following the Last Supper. The authors of the Gospels offer little comment on the reasons why Jesus washed the feet of His disciples, but the changes in the verse made in the JST provide the reason that it was to fulfill a Jewish law: "Jesus saith to him, He that *has* washed *his hands and his head* needeth not save to wash his feet, but is clean every whit: and ye are clean, but not all. *Now this was the custom of the Jews under their law: wherefore, Jesus did this that the law might be fulfilled*" (JST John 13:10; italics indicate changes to the KJV text).

A JST change to the Gospel of Mark has received little

attention over the years because it was not included in the footnotes of printed Latter-day Saint editions of the Bible. It offers an intriguing insight into the motives of Judas Iscariot that are found nowhere else in the Bible or in other scriptural writings. It suggests that Judas Iscariot was offended on the night of the Last Supper and that he heard the prophecy of his betrayal and understood the intent. The changed verse reads: "But after that I am risen, I will go before you into Galilee. *And he said unto Judas Iscariot, what thou doest, do quickly; but beware of innocent blood. Nevertheless, Judas Iscariot, even one of the twelve, went unto the chief priests to betray Jesus unto them; for he turned away from him, and was offended because of his words. And when the chief priests heard of him, they were glad, and promised to give him money; and he sought how he might conveniently betray Jesus*" (JST Mark 14:28; italics indicate changes to the KJV text).

STUDY QUESTIONS

1. The Last Supper was a private meal with Jesus and His disciples and possibly a number of other close friends and followers. What differences in the tone of Jesus's teachings during the Last Supper do you see from His public teachings?

2. If Jesus took upon Himself our sins, mistakes, hurts, and disappointments, how can we truly *give* them to Him and move on with our lives?

3. Think specifically about the Last Supper during the next sacrament service you attend. How is partaking of the bread and water like being present at the Last Supper?

CHAPTER 34

THE TRIAL AND CONDEMNATION

Following Jesus's arrest by Roman soldiers and temple police (John 18:3, in which the Greek term translated "band of men" refers to a detachment of Roman soldiers), He was taken to the private residence of Annas, who was formerly the high priest and father-in-law to the current high priest, Caiaphas. In *Jesus the Christ,* Elder Talmage details the illegalities of the Jewish trial, in which Jesus was interrogated and accused of various crimes. Elder Talmage based his conclusions on the nineteenth-century scholarship he used in preparing his work. Scholars today realize that the Jewish sources used by earlier scholars to identify the illegalities of the trial come from a later period than the New Testament and, therefore, likely do not give an accurate portrayal of first-century Jewish practice. The Gospels do not accuse the Jewish council of illegalities, so we assume there were none to report. The hearing before the Jewish leaders is generally understood today as a fact-finding effort of the Roman judicial system, which routinely used local magistrates and administrators as part of their judicial process.

From a historical perspective, a Roman administrator may have asked the Jewish leadership to participate in initial hearings, and Pilate orchestrated or approved the arrest, Jewish hearing, Roman trial, and crucifixion. The person who went to the Jewish leaders may not necessarily have been Pilate, who appears to have become involved when the interrogation of Jesus revealed that, potentially, a capital crime had been committed.

While Jesus was in the house of Annas, two of His disciples entered the home and watched as He was interrogated and abused. One of those men was Peter (John 18:16); the other was a disciple of Jesus known to Caiaphas (John 18:15). The Jewish interrogators reflected an intense interest in generating a legal charge that was punishable under Roman law. Matthew depicts the evening as starting at that point and ending on a bitter note as Jesus's assailants turned violent toward him (Matthew 26:57–68). Roman courts and Jewish courts were not interested in the same crimes. A charge of blasphemy, which was punishable in a Jewish court, had little weight in a Roman court. The many witnesses who came forward against Jesus may have struggled to generate a charge that was punishable in a Roman court.

Eventually, a charge was brought forward that had staying power: "This fellow said, I am able to destroy the temple of God, and to build it in three days" (Matthew 26:61). The charge sup-posedly expressed Jesus's hostility toward a public institution and against Rome's ability to protect the public peace. Very probably no one that evening took the charge literally or believed that Jesus was actually a threat to the temple, but it was something to which the Roman governor would listen. After a beating, Jesus was led away to Pilate for punishment (Matthew 26:67; 27:2).

According to Gospel sources, Jesus was already condemned by the time He was delivered to Pilate, who never carried out his own investigation but simply asked whether Jesus had any defense to offer against the charges. Jesus declined to defend Himself. The speed with which Pilate dispatched the case is not surprising or noteworthy by first-century standards, and the fact that Jesus was dead in only a few hours of having His case heard by a Roman governor is not surprising. Once Jesus was in his custody, Pilate made a few calculated decisions that helped him determine whether he should put Jesus to death or whether he should let Him go.

We have no historical evidence that Pilate favored either side in the trial of Jesus; instead, he merely heard the case of a man who was accused of a trumped-up crime by the leading Jewish authorities with whom he had had a fairly turbulent relationship. When Pilate chose to offer up a vote on the release of one of two prisoners, either Jesus of Nazareth or Barabbas, Pilate may simply have been trying to determine whether Caiaphas and his men were in the majority or whether the followers of Jesus were in the majority.

The release of Barabbas, portrayed as a great irony by Matthew (see below), proved that the voices against Jesus were louder than those against Barabbas. The release of Barabbas says nothing about his perceived guilt or innocence. Pilate then sent Jesus to Herod Antipas to determine the issue of jurisdiction. Because Jesus was from Nazareth, which is in Galilee, Herod Antipas held jurisdiction over Him and technically should have taken Jesus into his custody. During His interrogation under Antipas, Jesus refused to speak. Finally, Jesus was sent back to Pilate, who had Jesus scourged and preparations made for His crucifixion.

Since 1915

Jesus Barabbas. According to all four Gospels, Pontius Pilate presented Jesus and another condemned criminal to the crowd, one of whom would be granted his freedom in a tradition associated with Passover. The crowd chose to release Barabbas, who was likely named Jesus Barabbas. Some ancient Greek manuscripts of the New Testament preserve the entire name of Jesus Barabbas. Ironically, Pilate had before him two men, one named Jesus the son of the father (Jesus Bar-Abbas) and the other, Jesus the divine Son of the Father.

Yohanan ossuary. An ossuary, or a stone box for bones, was found containing the bones of a crucified victim in 1968 at Giv'at ha-mivtar, a suburb of modern Jerusalem. The outside inscription identifies the man as Yohanan (John), executed in the first century—the only example of a first-century victim of crucifixion. The central discovery is an anklebone with a spike protruding through it and pieces of olive wood, indicating that the victim was attached to a wooden beam.

Joseph Smith Translation

The New Testament preserves two traditions about Judas's death (Matthew 27:3–5 and Acts 1:18–19). Matthew in the Joseph Smith Translation harmonizes the two accounts: "Then Judas, *who* had betrayed him, when he saw that he was condemned, repented himself, and brought again the thirty pieces of silver to the chief priests and elders, Saying, I have sinned in that I have betrayed the innocent blood. And they said *unto him,* What is that to us? See thou to it; *thy sins be upon thee.* And he cast down the pieces of silver in the temple, and departed, and went and hanged himself *on a tree. And straightway he fell down, and his bowels gushed out, and he died. And therefore they took the pieces of silver,* and gave them for the potter's field, as the Lord appointed *by the mouth of Jeremy*" (JST Matthew 27:3–5, 10; italics indicate changes to the KJV text).

STUDY QUESTIONS

1. How do we condemn people unfairly? What can we do to avoid doing so in the future?
2. Identify a time when you changed your opinion of someone because you pushed aside your prejudice. How were you able to do so? How did it make you feel when you did?

CHAPTER 35

DEATH AND BURIAL

Unfortunately, we do not know the precise whereabouts of the praetorium, or judgment hall, where Jesus was scourged and sent toward Calvary (see John 18:28), but the distance to the site of the Crucifixion was likely not very great. The Crucifixion, wherever it was held, undoubtedly occurred on one of the main roads into the city, where Rome intentionally placed the crosses of crucifixion so they would act as a strong visible deterrent to future crime. From the site of the scourging, Jesus was required to carry the top beam of the cross to the place of crucifixion; the upright beam was most likely already fixed in the ground at the site. Somewhere along the route to the Crucifixion, Jesus's physical body gave out, and He was no longer able to carry His cross. A man named Simon of Cyrene was enlisted to carry the beam the rest of the way.

When we understand the brutalities Jesus suffered—the agony of Gethsemane, beatings, scourging, and a night without sleep—we can understand that death by crucifixion would have been relatively quick. After those in charge had inflicted so many traumas upon His body, they had little expectation that He would live long on the cross. Jesus was crucified sometime around 9 A.M. on Friday, and He was dead by the early afternoon, around 3 P.M. Shortly before His death, He spoke to His Father: "Eli, Eli, lama sabachthani? that is to say, My God, my God, why hast thou forsaken me?" (Matthew 27:46). From approximately 3 P.M. until just before sundown, Jesus's body hung on the cross. Near sundown, His body was taken down and prepared for burial.

According to John, two men stepped forward to receive the body of Jesus: Nicodemus and Joseph of Arimathea, both of whom were leaders of the Jews in Jerusalem. They washed His body, wrapped it, and laid it in a tomb—all before the beginning of the Sabbath. Because they were rushed in their preparations, the two men washed and wrapped it but did not finish anointing it with spices, such as aloe.

Modern prophets and apostles see the Atonement as a culmination of three intertwined events: the prayer and suffering in Gethsemane, the Crucifixion, and the Resurrection. Those three events in sequence constitute the Atonement. In its most basic sense, the word *atonement* is used to translate a Greek word that means "to reconcile accounts" or "agree to settle debts." In a very real sense, through those three events, Jesus paid the price of sin. The Gospels do not highlight the agony Jesus suffered, but the accounts clearly show that He suffered profound pain and heartbreak.

SINCE 1915

The day of the Crucifixion. To the modern reader, the time that Jesus spent in the tomb can be rather confusing because

Matthew 12 seems to indicate that Jesus was in the tomb for three days *and* three nights: "For as Jonas was three days and three nights in the whale's belly; so shall the Son of man be three days and three nights in the heart of the earth" (Matthew 12:40). From a technical perspective, Jesus was in the tomb by Friday evening, and He was already resurrected by Sunday morning, which hardly seems to fulfill the prophecy that the entombment would last three days and three nights.

Although we cannot explain the issue of three nights, we can point out that by Jewish calculations, Jesus did spend a portion of three days in the tomb. By Jewish calculations, a day begins at sundown each day, and thus Jesus spent part of the first day (Friday evening before sundown) in the tomb, a complete twenty-four-hour day in the tomb (Friday at sundown to Saturday at sundown), and a portion of a third day in the tomb (Saturday at sundown until the time of the Resurrection sometime Sunday).

The practice of crucifixion. Crucifixion in first-century Judea was a brutal practice that was intentionally humiliating. In that respect, Jesus's Crucifixion was like every other crucifixion carried out in the region. Individuals were routinely nailed to the cross with nails in their hands and/or wrists and in their feet; the practice of tying individuals to a cross was unusual and is largely a modern invention. The name of the crime of the person being crucified was affixed to the cross somewhere, and Jesus's so-called crime was "THIS IS JESUS THE KING OF THE JEWS" (Matthew 27:37). Because of the Jewish prohibition against leaving the dead out on the Sabbath, Rome permitted Jewish crucifixion victims to have their legs broken so they would die before nightfall and their bodies could thus be taken down that day. Because of the rapidity with which individuals died after having their legs broken on the cross, scholars assume that crucifixion affected breathing; thus, the individuals suffocated in part from the weight of their hanging bodies.

"**Thou shalt be with me in paradise.**" In the Gospel of Luke, Jesus spoke to one of two criminals being crucified beside Him: "And Jesus said unto him, Verily I say unto thee, To day shalt thou be with me in paradise" (Luke 23:43). Modern Latter-day Saint readers have a difficult time reading this verse without interjecting into it all of their modern understanding of what paradise means and including in the definition of the word all that the Restoration has revealed about the world of spirits.

When Jesus spoke these words, the idea of paradise was loosely defined as a place where the righteous dead went after death. The Jews had only recently come to understand that the wicked and righteous were separated at death and that paradise was something akin to what Christians would later call heaven. From Jewish writings at the time, we learn that many Jews apparently felt that only the very righteous, such as the prophets and great men of their day, would enter paradise. Some would have mocked the suggestion that anyone except the very righteous could enter paradise, and we see here that Jesus had a different definition of paradise and of who would go there.

The time of Jesus's death. A slight discrepancy occurs in the exact time of Jesus's Crucifixion. In the Gospel of Mark, Jesus is crucified at 9 A.M. (Mark 15:25). From noon until 3 P.M., darkness prevailed (Mark 15:33). Jesus died shortly after 3 P.M. (Mark 15:37). Luke follows the same time frame.

In John 19:14, however, Jesus was still before Pilate at the sixth hour of the day; therefore, He could not have been crucified until noon. For John, the sixth hour, high noon, is significant. The Samaritan woman met Jesus at noon and came to know of His mission. For John, Jesus's death at the sixth hour corresponded to the height of the sun at noonday that came when Jesus died. Obviously, however, the hour of Jesus's death is less important than the reasons for His death.

JOSEPH SMITH'S TEACHINGS

Matthew 27:1. "Darkness prevails at this time as it was at the time Jesus Christ was about to be crucified. The powers of darkness strove to obscure the glorious sun of righteousness that began to dawn upon the world and was soon to burst in great blessings upon the heads of the faithful" (Jessee, Ashurst-McGee, and Jensen, eds., *Journals, Volume 1:1832–1839,* 96; see also The Joseph Smith Papers, accessed 8 July 2014, http://josephsmith papers.org/paperSummary/journal-1835-1836?p=32).

JOSEPH SMITH TRANSLATION

The Joseph Smith Translation offers a minor correction that appears to deal with the issue of culpability for the death of Jesus. While on the cross, Jesus asked the Father to "forgive them; for they know not what they do." It appears from these words that the request for forgiveness was for those who carried out the Crucifixion itself but did not include everyone who was involved with the Crucifixion. Again, the JST offers clarity. It specifies precisely whom Jesus intended. Following the word *do* in the above quotation, the JST adds, "(meaning the soldiers who crucified him)" (JST Luke 23:34).

STUDY QUESTIONS

1. What did you learn about Joseph of Arimathea in this chapter? About Nicodemus? About Mary Magdalene? How can you apply what you learned about them in your own life?
2. What thoughts and feelings does the Crucifixion of the Lord

bring to mind? How do these thoughts and feelings shape our relationship with Him?

3. What lessons can we learn from the way that Jesus treated the two bandits who were also crucified on the same day as He was?

CHAPTER 36

IN THE REALM OF
DISEMBODIED SPIRITS

The ministry of the Lord Jesus Christ in the world of spirits, although receiving only passing attention in the New Testament, is a vital part of the doctrine of performing vicarious work for the dead in modern temples.

In this chapter, Elder Talmage sets forth the doctrine of the redemption of the dead and the role of modern temples in redeeming the dead. He was well qualified to discuss this important aspect of Jesus's ministry because he wrote the first book-length study of modern temple worship, *The House of the Lord,* three years before completing *Jesus the Christ.*

Elder Talmage declares, "Christ's atoning sacrifice was offered, not alone for the few who lived upon the earth while He was in the flesh, nor for those who were to be born in mortality after His death, but for all inhabitants of the earth then, past, present, and future" (676). This great truth helps solve the apparent conflict in a belief that God is love, the necessity of accepting Christ for salvation, and the fact that a large majority of God's children were born at a time when and in a place where the gospel was not preached.

Elder Talmage's understanding, like that of other Latter-day Saints at the time, was limited regarding Christ's specific labors in the spirit world because the most complete revelation on the subject had not yet been received.

SINCE 1915

Vision of the redemption of the dead. In October 1918, three years after *Jesus the Christ* was published, President Joseph F. Smith received a vision, known today as the vision of the redemption of the dead (recorded in Doctrine and Covenants 138). Our understanding of what Jesus did in the spirit world has been greatly enhanced by the new light and knowledge received by President Smith. Specifically, we learn from the vision of the redemption of the dead that Jesus did not go in person to the wicked and disobedient but instead sent His chosen messengers to them (Doctrine and Covenants 138:20–22, 29), a singular insight not reflected in *Jesus the Christ.*

Spirit prison. Traditionally, many Latter-day Saints consider the world of spirits as being divided into two separate spheres, paradise and prison. Following the reception of the vision of the redemption of the dead in October 1918, it became clear that the entire spirit world is a prison for all those who have died—captured by death and held there until resurrection.

The vision of the redemption of the dead indicates that the "spirits of the just, who had been faithful in the testimony of Jesus" inhabit the world of spirits, which is divided into two places. The first sphere is where the righteous awaited "deliverance," "redemption from the bands of death," and "deliverance from the chains of death." It was here that Christ appeared to declare "liberty to the captives" and where at the time of His visit they "rejoiced in their redemption . . . [and] acknowledged the Son of God as their Redeemer and Deliverer from death and the chains of hell" (Doctrine and Covenants 138:15–18, 23). The second sphere is where the wicked, ungodly, and unrepentant awaited "messengers, clothed with power and authority, and commissioned" to teach them the gospel and "vicarious baptism" (Doctrine and Covenants 138:30, 33).

JOSEPH SMITH'S TEACHINGS

Luke 23:42–43. "I will say something about the spirits in prison. There has been much said about the saying of Jesus on the cross to the thief, saying, 'This day thou shalt be with me in paradise.' The commentators or translators make it out to say 'paradise,' but what is 'paradise'? It is a modern word; it does not answer at all to the original that Jesus made use of. There is nothing in the original, in any language, that signifies 'paradise.' But it was 'This day I will be with thee in the world of spirits and will teach thee, or answer thy inquiries.' The thief on the cross was to be with Jesus Christ in the world of spirits. He did not say 'paradise' or 'heaven.' . . .

"There has been also much said about the word 'hell,' and the sectarian world have preached much about it. But what is hell? It is another modern term. It is taken from *hadēs*, the Greek, or *she'ôl*, the Hebrew. The true signification is a world of spirits. *Hadēs, she'ôl*, paradise, spirits in prison—[it] is all one. It is a world of spirits. The righteous and the wicked all go to the same world of spirits" (Discourse, 11 June 1843, recorded by Wilford Woodruff, as cited in Jackson, *Joseph Smith's Commentary*, 128).

1 Peter 3:18–19; 4:6. "Here then we have an account of our

Savior preaching to the spirits in prison, to spirits that had been imprisoned from the days of Noah. And what did he preach to them? That they were to stay there? Certainly not. Let his own declaration testify; 'he hath sent me to heal the broken hearted, to preach deliverance to the captives, and recovering of sight to the blind, to set at liberty them that are bruised' (Luke 4:18). Isaiah has it, 'to bring out the prisoners from the prison, and them that sit in darkness from the prison house' (Isaiah 42:7). It is very evident from this that he not only went to preach to them but to deliver, or bring them out of the prison house. . . . Those who were disobedient in the days of Noah were visited by our Savior, who possessed the everlasting Melchizedek Priesthood, and had the gospel preached to them by him in prison. And in order that they might fulfill all the requisitions of God, their living friends were baptized for their dead friends and thus fulfilled the requirements of God" ("Baptism for the Dead," *Times and Seasons,* 15 April 1842, 760–61).

Joseph Smith Translation

The Joseph Smith Translation changes in 1 Peter make explicit what the King James Version implies: "For Christ also once suffered for sins, the just for the unjust, being put to death in the flesh, but quickened by the Spirit, *that he might bring us to God: For* which *cause* also he went and preached unto the spirits in prison; *some of whom* were disobedient in the days of Noah, *while the longsuffering of God waited,* while the ark was preparing, wherein few, that is, eight souls were saved by water" (JST 1 Peter 3:18–20; italics indicate changes to the KJV text).

STUDY QUESTIONS

1. How was Christ's ministry in the spirit world a continuation of His earthly ministry?

2. In what ways does a knowledge of salvation for the dead help you understand God's love for all His children?

3. What truths have been added to our understanding of Christ's ministry in the world of spirits by President Joseph F. Smith's vision of the redemption of the dead?

CHAPTER 37

THE RESURRECTION
AND THE ASCENSION

During the events surrounding the Crucifixion and Resurrection, the disciples stayed in Jerusalem, no doubt afraid for their own safety and watchful that they too might be arrested and executed for the same crime of which Jesus was convicted. For whatever reasons, they did not anticipate that Jesus would be resurrected Sunday morning (Matthew 12:40). In any case, some of Jesus's female disciples and followers traveled to the tomb to finish caring for His body according to first-century Jewish burial customs.

To the women's surprise and astonishment, the tomb was empty, and they reported that information to the Apostles (John 20:2). Only Peter and John raced to see for themselves if the tomb was indeed empty. After they returned from visiting the tomb, Mary Magdalene remained at the site, weeping and worried at what had happened to the body of Jesus. At some point, the resurrected Jesus appeared to her, making her the first of all of

His followers to witness that He was indeed raised from the dead. In quick succession, Jesus also appeared to a number of other followers individually and in groups, both small and large.

The accounts are not necessarily in order of appearance, but we know that the following individuals were blessed to become witnesses of the Resurrection: Mary Magdalene near the sepulcher (Mark 16:9, 10; John 20:14); Jesus's female followers somewhere between the sepulcher and Jerusalem (Matthew 28:9); two disciples on the road to Emmaus (Mark 16:12; Luke 24:13); Peter, in or near Jerusalem (Luke 24:34; 1 Corinthians 15:5); ten of the Apostles and others at Jerusalem (Luke 24:36; John 20:19); the eleven Apostles at Jerusalem (Mark 16:14; John 20:26); the Apostles at the Sea of Tiberias, Galilee (John 21); the eleven Apostles on a mountain in Galilee (Matthew 28:16); five hundred brethren at once (1 Corinthians 15:6); His brother James (1 Corinthians 15:7); and the eleven Apostles at the time of the ascension (Mark 16:19; Luke 24:50, 51).

As at other times when the Lord revealed Himself physically to His followers, we find multiple accounts and multiple visits. In one instance, He visited "the eleven," who were all being prepared to be special witnesses of Christ (Mark 16:14). They became the foundation for the Church in Jesus's name. Paul relates sometime later that Jesus appeared to more than five hundred individuals, making them also witnesses of the Resurrection (1 Corinthians 15:6).

Elder Talmage concludes this chapter with a discussion of the "Final Commission and the Ascension" (695–97). Because the Gospels do not provide an exact, consistent chronological order of events in the ministry of Jesus Christ, authors attempt to provide readers a coherent chronology. Naturally, writers disagree on the order of some events mentioned in the Gospels, but these chronological disagreements do not substantially change what we know about the main events in the life of Christ.

In this last section, Elder Talmage associates the events found in Matthew 28, Mark 16, and Luke 24 as occurring at the end of the forty-day ministry (Acts 1:3), when the risen Lord ascended to heaven.

SINCE 1915

Claudius inscription. A large marble slab, dated AD 41–54, was found in Palestine with an imperial decree written in Greek that says, "It is my will that graves and tombs lie undisturbed forever. . . . I require that he be executed for tomb-robbery." This edict recalls Matthew's story concerning rumors circulating about Jesus's body: "Say ye, his disciples came by night, and stole him away while we slept. . . . And this saying is commonly reported among the Jews until this day" (cf. Matthew 28:11–15). This edict may have been a result of reports by faithful Saints of the Resurrection of Jesus.

JOSEPH SMITH'S TEACHINGS

Matthew 27:52–53. "We read that many bodies of the Saints arose at Christ's resurrection, probably all the Saints" (*Times and Seasons,* 16 May 1841, 430).

Luke 24:46–47. "By this we learn that it behooved Christ to suffer and to be crucified and rise again on the third day, for the express purpose that repentance and remission of sins should be preached unto all nations" ("To the Elders of the Church of Latter Day Saints," *Messenger and Advocate,* September 1835, 180–81, as cited in Jackson, *Joseph Smith's Commentary,* 128).

Joseph Smith Translation

Historically speaking, when Jesus met with Mary Magdalene in the garden of the empty tomb, He did not say to her "Touch me not," as the King James Version renders the passage. Other translations of the Bible render the verse in a variety of different ways that try to capture the nuance of the verse, which says literally, "Do not hold me back" or "Do not hold on to me." Although the Prophet Joseph Smith did not read Greek or have access to other translations of the Bible, his inspired translation of this verse captures better than the King James Version the meaning of the Greek text: "Jesus saith unto her, *Hold* me not; for I am not yet ascended to my Father: but go to my brethren, and say unto them, I ascend unto my Father, and your Father; and to my God, and your God" (JST John 20:17; italics indicate changes to the KJV text).

Study Questions

1. What is the basis of your personal testimony regarding the Resurrection?
2. How could your belief in and testimony of the Resurrection affect your relationship with family members? With co-workers? With people at Church? With people you see each day?
3. Can you believe in something you have not seen, touched, heard, or smelled? If so, how is that possible?

CHAPTER 38

THE APOSTOLIC MINISTRY

Elder Talmage discusses some of the most important events noted in the book of Acts and then concludes this chapter with a brief discussion regarding John's vision found in the book of Revelation.

Among the important events mentioned by Luke in the book of Acts were the calling of Matthias to replace Judas Iscariot (Acts 1:15–26), the bestowal of the Holy Ghost (Acts 2), the death of Stephen and his vision of the Lord (Acts 6), and Saul's vision on the road to Damascus and his call to preach the gospel to the Gentiles (Acts 9).

Elder Talmage then notes, "The period of apostolic ministry continued until near the close of the first century of our era, approximately sixty to seventy years from the time of the Lord's ascension" (716).

The fate of Jesus's early Apostles is not known with confidence, except in the case of James, who was killed by Herod (Acts

12:1–2). Likely we should accept the early stories about Peter and Paul dying in Rome. Later legendary stories about their deaths that became part of Christian lore, however, should most likely be disregarded. What we do know with some degree of confidence is that all the earliest disciples remained true to their faith and that nearly all of them suffered martyrdom for it. Those early disciples established a pattern of spreading the good news of the gospel to the world despite physical hardship and even death.

SINCE 1915

The deaths of Stephen and James in Jerusalem. The deaths of Stephen and James in Jerusalem reveal that the Jews did, in reality, inflict the death penalty on individuals. Killing Christian leaders was a deliberate attempt to stop the growth of Christianity. The book of Acts shows, however, that killing these leaders did not successfully slow down the growth of the Christian church during this period. Stephen was stoned, and a few years later, in AD 44, Herod Agrippa ordered the beheading of James.

The God-fearers. One of the topics Elder Talmage does not address in this chapter was the conversion of Cornelius, who was a God-fearer (Acts 10). Our understanding of the relationship between God-fearers and proselytes has increased significantly since 1915. Generally, a proselyte is defined as a convert to Judaism, fully submitting to the Jewish requirement to be circumcised and to a life dedicated to obeying the Mosaic requirements of the Torah. The description "God-fearer," on the other hand, may generally apply to a Gentile who accepted Yahweh (Jehovah) as the only true and living God and observed some of the Mosaic requirements but had not specifically submitted to circumcision. Luke highlighted their presence in several instances in the book of Acts, identifying the important role God-fearers played during the first stages of the Gentile missionary effort, beginning with Peter's visit to Cornelius in Caesarea Maritima.

The loss of Apostles. At some point, most likely by the end of the first century, the office of Apostle had ceased to exist. Recently scholars have suggested that the Apostles' twofold calling in the New Testament as witnesses of the Resurrection and as having actually walked with Jesus when He was alive made the calling unique and therefore of a finite duration. The New Testament does not record any instructions on the cessation of the office, but it does record the special requirements for the Apostle who would fill the position Judas held (Acts 1:21–22). Restoration scripture informs us that the deaths of the Apostles resulted in the loss of the keys of apostleship—one of the principal results of the Apostasy, which took place during the first century. The Lord, however, has called modern Apostles, known as "special witnesses of the name of Christ in all the world" (Doctrine and Covenants 107:23). This office continues today in the Restored Church, which is The Church of Jesus Christ of Latter-day Saints.

JOSEPH SMITH'S TEACHINGS

Acts 1:4–5. "When the apostles were raised up, they worked in Jerusalem, and Jesus commanded them to tarry there until they were endowed with power from on high. Had they not work to do in Jerusalem? They did work and prepared the people for the Pentecost. The kingdom of God was with them before the day of Pentecost, as well as afterwards. . . . The endowment was to prepare the disciples for their mission into the world" (Discourse, 22 January 1843, recorded by Wilford Woodruff, as cited in Jackson, *Joseph Smith's Commentary,* 143).

Acts 7:55–56. "Stephen saw the Son of Man. [He] saw the Son of Man standing on the right hand of God. [There are] three personages in heaven who hold the keys—one to preside over all. (Discourse, 11 June 1843, recorded by Willard Richards, as cited in Jackson, *Joseph Smith's Commentary,* 148; see also Ehat and Cook, *Words of Joseph Smith,* 212).

"Jesus Christ sat on the right hand of God. Any person that has seen the heavens opened knows that there are three personages in the heavens holding the keys of power" (Discourse, 11 June 1843, recorded by Wilford Woodruff, as cited in Jackson, *Joseph Smith's Commentary,* 148; see also Ehat and Cook, *Words of Joseph Smith,* 214).

Acts 9:3–6. "Jesus himself, when he appeared to Paul on his way to Damascus, did not inform him how he could be saved. . . . Paul could not learn so much from the Lord relative to his duty in the common salvation of man, as he could from one of Christ's ambassadors, called with the same heavenly calling of the Lord, and endowed with the same power from on high so that what they loosed on earth, should be loosed in heaven; and what they bound on earth should be bound in heaven: He, the Lord being a priest for ever, after the order of Melchizedek [Psalm 110:4] and the anointed son of God, from before the foundation of the world, and they the begotten sons of Jesus through the gospel" ("Baptism," *Times and Seasons,* 1 September 1842, 905).

JOSEPH SMITH TRANSLATION

The book of Acts contains three separate accounts of Jesus's appearing to Paul on the road to Damascus (Acts 9:4–7; 22:7–9; 26:14–16). Slight differences are found in two of the accounts, which the Joseph Smith Translation harmonizes: "And *they who were journeying* with him *saw indeed the light, and were afraid; but they heard not the* voice *of him who spake to him*" (JST Acts 9:7; italics indicate changes from the KJV text).

Study Questions

1. What things in your life prevent you from receiving a confirmation that the Lord has called someone to His work?

2. What can you do now to enjoy the Holy Ghost more fully in your life?

3. The growth of the early Christian church was explosive in many aspects. What parallels do you see between the growth of the Church in the first century AD and the growth of the Church in the nineteenth century AD?

CHAPTER 39

MINISTRY OF THE RESURRECTED CHRIST ON THE WESTERN HEMISPHERE

In this chapter, Elder Talmage carefully reviews Jesus Christ's visit to the Nephites, as recorded in the Book of Mormon. This visit is fundamentally different from His visits to the people of Jerusalem and Galilee, in part because the wicked among the Nephites had been destroyed, so He appeared in the New World to a small gathering of the faithful who were ready to receive Him.

The book of 3 Nephi is devoted to Christ's appearance in the New World, and many of the teachings found in the Gospels can be found in 3 Nephi as well, notably the Sermon on the Mount (3 Nephi 12–14) and many teachings from the Gospel of John. As He had done in the Old World, Jesus organized His followers in the New World. He established a group of twelve disciples who would lead the Church in His absence, and He taught them to meet together and pray in His name:

"And behold, ye shall meet together oft; and ye shall not

forbid any man from coming unto you when ye shall meet to-gether, but suffer them that they may come unto you and forbid them not" (3 Nephi 18:22). Also, "The church did meet together oft, to fast and to pray, and to speak one with another concerning the welfare of their souls" (Moroni 6:5).

Without focusing on what Jesus taught but on how He taught, we can conclude that the Church in the New World was patterned in the same way as the Church in the Old World. The Lord called His faithful to lead the Church, and He required them to rely on Him for continuing inspiration and guidance.

Sometimes in teaching the Apostasy of the early Christian church, we give the impression that it was complete and abso-lute and that no inspiration was given after a certain point in time. But perhaps the situation among the Nephites can help us understand that the slide into apostasy is gradual and cycli-cal rather than absolute and fixed. Among the Nephites, the swing from apostasy to faith and back to apostasy was gradual and almost constant throughout their history. The short book of 4 Nephi documents the total conversion of the Nephites and the Lamanites and their eventual fall into apostasy. Much can be said of the history of Christianity in the Roman world, where the Church fell into apostasy and then attempted to renew its original faith only to eventually fall again. Apostasy in its most fundamental meaning is a mutiny, in which people rebel against lawful authority. The forces of rebellion are constantly in motion in all societies.

Since 1915

Lamanites. Over the course of the past nearly two hundred years, members of the Church of Jesus Christ have grown in their understanding of who the Lamanites were and what relationship the native peoples in North, Central, and South America may have to the people of the Book of Mormon.

In the first decades after the organization of the Church, members in general assumed that all native peoples in North, Central, and South America were descendants of the Lehites. At that time, little understanding existed of the vast differences in ethnicity among indigenous American peoples. Over time, as Church membership grew and expanded into so-called Lamanite territories, the Church began to recognize that the earlier, simple definition was insufficient.

Today the most recent edition of the Book of Mormon contains a change in the introduction that reflects the Church's current understanding of the identity of the Lamanites. It reads, "After thousands of years, all were destroyed except the Lamanites, and they are among the ancestors of the American Indians." Previous editions of the Book of Mormon had implied that all American Indians were Lamanites, but the newest edition limits that statement considerably.

Joseph Smith's Teachings

"Take away the Book of Mormon, and the revelations, and where is our religion? We have none" (21 April 1834, Kirtland High Council Minute Book, 44, Church History Library, The Church of Jesus Christ of Latter-day Saints, Salt Lake City, Utah).

Study Questions

1. What events characterize the Lord's visit to the Nephites? How was His visit to them different from His appearances in the Old World?

2. What particular story or incident during Christ's visit to the New World helps you appreciate the gospel more?

3. What is a broken heart? What is a contrite spirit? How can we experience both more deeply?

CHAPTER 40

THE LONG NIGHT
OF APOSTASY

You should remember while reading this chapter that Elder Talmage drew upon Protestant scholarship in recounting the historical development of early Christianity following the close of the New Testament. Protestants have typically been quite critical of the development of Christianity after the start of the fourth century—or after the rise of the Roman Catholic Church in the West. Orthodox, or Eastern, Christianity, a much longer tradition, rarely was acknowledged or discussed by Protestants.

For many reasons, Protestants have seen the fourth through seventeenth centuries as a long period of darkness. Seldom did they acknowledge any good arising during this period. But the Western Christian church did provide a place for the poor and powerless to find some justice. It also provided educational opportunities, hospitality, and medical help in the wake of the fall of the Roman empire in the West, which left an administrative vacuum. The church abolished slavery and crucifixion. It provided, through a religious calendar punctuated with holy days, some respite from constant work, which before that time had begun at sunrise and lasted into the evening seven days a week. Monks and scribes copied and preserved biblical texts, one of the greatest legacies. The list of contributions of Western Christianity is numerous during this period despite its inability to preserve the doctrine taught by the Apostles, which had been lost long before the establishment of the Catholic Church (Acts 2:42).

Today, Latter-day Saint leaders do not single out specific churches as apostate, nor do they emphasize a particular historical development in Christianity as apostate. Instead, our growing understanding of religious history helps us see that apostasy in some form has always been present and that the forces of apostasy, personal and institutional, have always been at work. Indeed, a very real apostasy occurred, but the greater threat remains personal and not historical.

In light of the new emphasis, we may want to consider actions that are apostate rather than institutions that are apostate. In this chapter, some apostate actions and attitudes mentioned specifically by Elder Talmage include (1) corruption of the simple doctrines of the gospel of Christ by admixture with so-called philosophic systems, (2) unauthorized additions to the prescribed rites of the Church and the introduction of significant alterations in essential ordinances, and (3) unauthorized changes in Church organization and government. To this list, we might recognize universal causes: pride and the desire for power and authority.

Since 1915

Christian councils and creeds. The earliest Church council is recorded in Acts 15 when the Apostles and elders met to discuss the matter of whether Gentile converts needed to be circumcised and maintain kosher eating standards if they were to be accepted into full fellowship in the Church (Acts 15).

Later, without Apostles and the guidance of the Holy Spirit (Acts 15:28), approximately fifteen hundred councils were held. Most of the complete official records of these councils have been lost; only about a dozen or so are still available to be read and studied.

Some of the important councils, beginning in the fourth century, came about at the behest of the Roman emperor to determine doctrine (earlier gatherings are more precisely identified as conferences not focused on doctrine but on internal issues regarding Church government). Recent academic studies demonstrate a significant shift in how the later councils functioned in comparison to the model found in Acts 15. Called or authorized by the emperor, the bishops decided issues based on a majority vote, which consensus was sometimes arrived at or enforced by violent actions. Most likely, the intent of earliest creeds was to provide a basic belief statement based primarily on scripture and traditions. As the centuries passed, more and more Church councils met and prepared statements announcing official positions. In the end, once Protestants separated themselves from the Roman Catholic Church, they no longer accepted the decisions made by these councils, and many groups issued confessions of faith instead. Since then, various Protestant groups, such as the Church of Christ and Disciples of Christ, have rejected these creeds or are ambivalent about whether the earliest creeds should be considered definitive statements of faith (such as those of the various Baptist churches).

Joseph Smith remembered Jesus Christ saying "that all their creeds were an abomination in his sight" (Joseph Smith–History 1:19). This condemnation appears to refer to the totality of the efforts to establish a creedal religion, which often focused more on what people believed than on how they lived or practiced Jesus's teachings.

Apostasy. The Greek word translated as *apostasy* in English means "revolt," "revolution," or "mutiny." *Apostasy,* as used in the New Testament, is a rebellion against the authority and revelations of God. It began during the lifetime of the Apostles and replaced the authority of the Apostles and their doctrine by the end of the first century. Instead of our looking for the Apostasy in later generations of Christians, the New Testament indicates that it occurred during the first century. What followed was the attempt by individuals and groups to understand and practice Christianity without authorized prophetic leaders. Nevertheless, the period following the close of the New Testament and the beginning of the Restoration was a time when courageous men and women of deep faith attempted to preserve, translate, and publish, as best they could, the holy scriptures—a marvelous blessing to us today. These men and women kept alive the flame of faith in God and in His Divine Son in a very dark and dangerous world until the time was right for the coming of the Father and the Son to initiate the restoration of all things.

Joseph Smith's Teachings

Matthew 13:24–43. "Now we learn by this parable not only the setting up of the kingdom in the days of the Savior, which is represented by the good seed which produced fruit, but also the corruptions of the Church, which are represented by the tares which were sown by the enemy, which his disciples would fain have plucked up, or cleansed the Church of, if their views had been favored by the Savior. But he, knowing all things, says, 'Not so,' as much as to say, 'Your views are not correct; the Church is in its infancy, and if you take this rash step, you will destroy the wheat, or the Church, with the tares. Therefore, it is better to let them grow together until the harvest, or the end of the world, which means the destruction of the wicked, which is not yet fulfilled.' . . .

"Now men cannot have any possible grounds to say that this is figurative, or that it does not mean what it says, for he is now explaining what he had previously spoken in parables. And according to this language, the end of the world is the destruction of the wicked. The harvest and the end of the world have an allusion directly to the human family in the last days—instead of the earth as many have imagined—and that which shall precede the coming of the Son of Man and the restitution of all things spoken of by the mouth of all the holy prophets since the world began. And the angels are to have something to do in this great work, for they are the reapers.

"As therefore the tares are gathered and burned in the fire, so shall it be in the end of this world. That is, as the servants of God go forth warning the nations, both priests and people, and as they harden their hearts and reject the light of the truth, these first being delivered over to the buffetings of Satan, and the law and the testimony being closed up as it was with the Jews, they are left in darkness and delivered over unto the day of burning. Thus, being bound up by their creeds and their bands made strong by their priests, [they] are prepared for the fulfillment of the saying of the Savior: 'The Son of man shall send forth his angels and gather out of his kingdom all things that offend, and them which do iniquity; and shall cast them into a furnace of fire, and there shall be wailing and gnashing of teeth.'

"We understand that the work of the gathering together of the wheat into barns, or garners, is to take place while the tares are being bound over and preparing for the day of burning, that after the day of burnings, 'the righteous shall shine forth like the sun in the kingdom of their Father. Who hath ears to hear, let him hear'" ("To the Elders of the Church of the Latter Day Saints," *Messenger and Advocate,* December 1835, 226–29, as cited in Jackson, *Joseph Smith's Commentary,* 94–95).

"God sows. The enemy comes and sows parties, divisions, and heresies. 'Shall we kill them?' 'No, not till harvest, the end of the world.' The Son of God will do as he ever has done from the beginning: send forth his angels. If the reapers do not come, the wheat cannot be saved. Nothing but [the] kingdom being restored can save the world" (Discourse, summer 1839, recorded by Willard Richards, "Pocket Companion," as cited in Jackson, *Joseph Smith's Commentary,* 95).

Joseph Smith Translation

The Joseph Smith Translation helps us understand the doctrine of the Apostasy as it was taught in the New Testament.

In 2 Thessalonians, two minor changes to the text help us better understand what ancient prophets taught about the Apostasy. The first reads, "Let no man deceive you by any means: for there *shall* come a falling away first, and that man of sin be revealed, the son of perdition" (JST 2 Thessalonians 2:3; italics indicate changes to the KJV text).

The second adds more detail and clarity: "For the mystery of iniquity doth already work *and he it is who now worketh, and Christ suffereth him to work,* until *the time is fulfilled that* he *shall* be taken out of the way. And then shall that wicked *one* be revealed, whom the Lord shall consume with the spirit of his mouth, and shall destroy with the brightness of his coming: *Yea, the Lord,* even *Jesus,* whose coming is *not until* after *there cometh a falling away,* *by* the working of Satan with all power and signs and lying wonders" (JST 2 Thessalonians 2:7–9; italics indicate changes to the KJV text).

STUDY QUESTIONS

1. How can we teach the principle of the Apostasy to our friends, family, and neighbors without being insensitive or offensive? How can we help our children and grandchildren avoid judging playmates and neighbors while still teaching them about the Apostasy?

2. What causes of apostasy among the Nephites and Lamanites are recorded in 4 Nephi? Are any of these discernable in your life?

3. In what way is individual apostasy more of a concern to us today than past institutional apostasy in Judaism or Christianity?

CHAPTER 41

PERSONAL MANIFESTATIONS OF GOD AND JESUS CHRIST IN MODERN TIMES

Elder Talmage introduces readers to a "new dispensation" through the story of the First Vision. Since 1915, when *Jesus the Christ* was first published, exciting discoveries have helped us broaden our understanding of the Restoration by providing us with more firsthand accounts of associated events. The Joseph Smith Papers Project continues to publish important volumes related to the early history of the Church as seen through the eyes of its first prophet. Along with a website, the project will eventually provide a complete record of all sources produced by Joseph Smith or under his direction.

The documents of the Restoration in the latter days, including the Book of Mormon, contain something that is rarely found in any other book of scripture—namely, firsthand accounts of visions, personal spiritual experiences, and the words spoken to individuals. Certainly previous dispensations have recorded the wording of revelations, but the record we have of those revelations shows them to be typically addressed to entire peoples and nations. Few revelations have been preserved that are based on firsthand accounts recorded at the time.

Having scriptural and historical details clarified by Restoration documents is a blessing, given that history recorded over centuries has a way of removing differences in primary sources. The four Gospels contain some minor differences in their accounts of events, such as whether Jesus was crucified at 9 A.M. or noon and whether Jesus's family already resided in Bethlehem or whether they traveled to Bethlehem from Nazareth.

The New Testament, for instance, presents a handful of accounts of Jesus's post-Resurrection appearances to His disciples. On the other hand, we have several firsthand accounts given by Joseph Smith of the First Vision and even more secondhand accounts of the same vision (lds.org "First Vision Accounts" presents a historical and doctrinal discussion of those accounts). We also have multiple copies of some sections of the Doctrine and Covenants, and we have portions of both the original Book of Mormon manuscript and the entirety of the printer's manuscript. All these sources provide depth and clarity to historical events, but they also require patience as we seek to understand the context in which events happened historically. These facts make the Restoration unique.

At its most basic level, the restoration of the gospel is profoundly different from other faiths because it is living and is built upon revelation. The Church, like the Savior, lives. Perhaps this was part of Joseph Smith's great declaration of the Restoration: "And now, after the many testimonies which have been given of him, this is the testimony, last of all, which we give of him: That he lives!" (Doctrine and Covenants 76:22).

In this short chapter, Elder Talmage also introduces the reader to the visitation of various angels, including Moroni (764–67), John the Baptist (767–68), and Peter, James, and John (768–69). Then he reviews the organization of the Church on 6 April 1830; the receipt of a heavenly vision recorded today in Doctrine and Covenants 76; and the appearance of Jesus Christ, Moses, and Elijah in the Kirtland Temple in 1836. He concludes the chapter with a discussion of "Jesus the Christ Is with His Church Today" (775–77).

Since 1915

Appearances of the Father and the Son. Elder Talmage highlights two appearances of the Father and the Son in the early days of the Restoration: in the First Vision in the spring of 1820 (Manchester, New York) and in a vision on 16 February 1832 (Hiram, Ohio). Additionally, he highlights the appearance of the Son on 3 April 1836 (Kirtland Temple). Recent research by Church historians has identified additional appearances, including the appearance of the Father and the Son on 3–6 June 1831 (Morley Farm in Ohio); again on 21 January 1836 (Kirtland Temple); and then on 28 January 1836 (Kirtland Temple).

Additionally, accounts have been recorded of the appearance of the Son in May 1831 (Smith family home, Manchester, New York); in March 1833 (Whitney Store, Kirtland, Ohio); on 18 December 1833 (Johnson Inn, Kirtland, Ohio); and on 21 January 1836 (Kirtland Temple), 28 January 1836 (Kirtland Temple), and 30 March 1836 (Kirtland Temple). Of course, these are not the only appearances of the Son in this, the last dispensation.

The First Vision. Elder Talmage quotes extensively from Joseph Smith's official account of the First Vision (758–63). This account, found in the Pearl of Great Price, was written for a non–Latter-day Saint audience sometime beginning in the spring of 1838. The earliest and most personal account is found in Joseph Smith–History, dated about 1832. In this early account, Joseph Smith recorded Jesus's first words to him: "Joseph my son, thy sins are forgiven thee. Go thy way walk in my statutes and keep my commandments. Behold I am the Lord of glory. I was crucified for the world that all those who believe on my name may have Eternal life" (Davidson, Whittaker, Jensen, and Ashurst-McGee, eds., *Histories, Volume 1: Joseph Smith Histories, 1832–1844,* 13; see also The Joseph Smith Papers, accessed 8 July 2014, http://josephsmithpapers.org/paperSummary /history-circa-summer-1832?p=3).

JOSEPH SMITH'S TEACHINGS

Matthew 24:14 (Joseph Smith–Matthew 1:31). "When [Matthew 24:14] is rightly understood, it will be edifying. . . . The Savior said, when those tribulations should take place, it should be committed to a man who should be a witness over the whole world. The keys of knowledge, power, and revelations should be revealed to a witness who should hold the testimony to the world. It has always been my province to dig up hidden mysteries, new things, for my hearers. Just at the time when some men think that I have no right to the keys of the priesthood, just at that time I have the greatest right. . . . All the testimony is that the Lord in the last days would commit the keys of the priesthood to a witness over all people. Has the gospel of the kingdom commenced in the last days? And will God take it from the man until he takes him himself? I have read it precisely as the words flowed from the lips of Jesus Christ. . . . John saw the angel having the holy priesthood who should preach the everlasting gospel to all nations [Revelation 14:6]. God had an angel, a special messenger, ordained and prepared for that purpose in the last days. Wo! Wo!

be to that man, or set of men, who lift up their hands against God and his witness in these last days. For they shall deceive almost the very chosen ones. . . . Every man who has a calling to minister to the inhabitants of the world was ordained to that very purpose in the Grand Council of Heaven before this world was. I suppose that I was ordained to this very office in that Grand Council" (Discourse, 12 May 1844, recorded by Thomas Bullock, as cited in Jackson, *Joseph Smith's Commentary,* 106–7; see also Ehat and Cook, *Words of Joseph Smith,* 366–67).

"Preached to a man who should be a witness to all people, is the meaning of the text" (Discourse, 12 May 1844, recorded by Samuel W. Richards, as cited in Jackson, *Joseph Smith's Commentary,* 107; see also Ehat and Cook, *Words of Joseph Smith,* 371).

STUDY QUESTIONS

1. We have several records of visitations of God the Father and His Son Jesus Christ during the early years of the Restoration. What did you learn from these visits, and how has knowing helped strengthen your faith?
2. Where have you found your own "grove"?
3. How can we prevent a sense of special privilege or superiority from affecting our behavior toward nonmembers of the Church of Jesus Christ?
4. Think about something good in Judaism, Islam, and Orthodox, Catholic, and Protestant Christianity. How can you enhance your own faith appropriately by applying what you admire in another faith tradition?

CHAPTER 42

JESUS THE CHRIST
TO RETURN

Finally, we should understand the importance of concluding the story by looking forward. In the living Church, we should perhaps realize the obvious fact that the living God guides and directs the work through living prophets and apostles. The return of Jesus Christ in glory represents this fundamental truth. The New Testament closes with the book of Revelation by looking forward to the return of the Lord in great glory and at a time of great calamity. The Book of Mormon closes by looking forward to a time of reunification when the prophets of their day will be reunited with us. The Restoration has no formal ending; it simply looks forward.

Elder Talmage indicates that the "second advent," or Second Coming of the Lord, is not to be understood as His personal appearance to select individuals or groups, such as to Saul of Tarsus on the road to Damascus or His appearance to the young Joseph Smith in the woodlands in western New York. Rather, the Second

Coming will occur at a time in the future when He will come in "power and great glory, accompanied by hosts of resurrected and glorified beings" to "inaugurate a reign of righteousness" (78).

Both Bible and Book of Mormon prophets and apostles prophesied of this day, and their inspired words are confirmed by modern revelation (783–85). The exact time of the Lord's coming has never been revealed, but Elder Talmage notes that "we are not left without definite information as to precedent signs" (785–86). The weight of scripture, both ancient and modern, is the "fact that the event is nigh at hand" (787). The kingdom of God, the restored Church, prepares the world for the coming of the kingdom of heaven. At that time, the Lord's Prayer, "Thy kingdom come. Thy will be done in earth, as it is in heaven" (Matthew 6:10), will be fulfilled, and Christ will inaugurate His thousand-year reign on earth (789–90). Eventually, after the Millennium, "Satan shall be loosed for a little season, and the final test of man's integrity to God shall ensue" (791).

At the end of this final time of testing, "Satan and his host" will be vanquished, and "the earth shall pass to its gloried and celestialized condition, and eternal abode for the exalted sons and daughters of God . . . redeemed, sanctified, and exalted through their Lord and God Jesus the Christ" (792).

Since 1915

The Millennium. The Millennium has been the subject of great interest over the years, but it was only alluded to in Jesus's teachings as preserved in the four Gospels. Instead, the revelation that established the doctrine of the Millennium was revealed many years after Christ's death when His remaining disciples were in difficult circumstances and were fearful for their lives. The book of Revelation is the most complete revelation on the Millennium, which means, literally, "a thousand years," and 1 Nephi 11–14 and Doctrine and Covenants 29, 45, 84, and 88 also contain significant revelations on the topic. We add to our understanding by remembering that the revelation establishing the doctrine was given as the Church entered an age of apostasy and the remaining Saints needed encouragement that eventual victory was assured, even though immediate victory was not.

Joseph Smith's Teachings

Matthew 24:36 (Joseph Smith–Matthew 1:40). "Christ says, 'No man knoweth the day or the hour when the Son of Man cometh.' . . . Did Christ speak this as a general principle throughout all generations? Oh no; he spoke in the present tense. No man that was then living upon the footstool of God knew the day or the hour. But he did not say that there was no man throughout all generations that should know the day or the hour. No, for this would be in flat contradiction with other scripture, for the prophet says that God will do nothing but what he will reveal unto his servants the prophets [Amos 3:7]. Consequently, if it is not made known to the prophets it will not come to pass" (Discourse, 6 April 1843, recorded by James Burgess, as cited in Jackson, *Joseph Smith's Commentary,* 112; see also Ehat and Cook, *Words of Joseph Smith,* 180–81).

Joseph Smith Translation

Although the Joseph Smith Translation makes a number of changes to the book of Revelation, many of the changes only slightly alter the meaning of what is already stated in the King James Version. For example, in the following change, the imagery of the KJV is made more vivid and explicit: "*For* behold, he cometh *in the* clouds; *with ten thousands of his saints in the kingdom, clothed with the glory of his Father.* And every eye shall see him, and they *who* pierced him: and all kindreds of the earth shall wail because of him. Even so, Amen" (Revelation 1:7; italics indicate changes to the KJV text).

A similar change also adds clarity and depth to a verse discussing the millennial reign of Christ: "And he shall rule them with *the word of God; and they shall be in his hands* as the vessels of *clay in the hands of* a potter; *and he shall govern them by faith, with equity and justice,* even as I received of my Father" (Revelation 2:27; italics indicate changes to the KJV text).

STUDY QUESTIONS

1. Why was it important for God to let us know that His Son is coming again?
2. What did you learn from Jesus's teachings about Matthew 24 that can help you feel less worried about the Second Coming?
3. If you knew that Christ would return this year, what changes would you make in your life now?
4. Identify one thing you are not currently doing that would help build the kingdom of God this coming year in preparation for the coming of the kingdom of heaven. What are you willing to do to incorporate what you know will help make a difference?

GLOSSARY

Abbreviations

adj. = adjective
adv. = adverb
n. = noun
pp. = past participle
ppr. = present participle
v. = verb

Terms

The following are modifications of definitions found in Noah Webster's 1828 dictionary, *American Dictionary of the English Language*.

Abased (pp.)—Reduced to a low state, humbled, degraded.

Abated (pp.)—Lessened; decreased; destroyed; mitigated.

Abhorrent (adj.)—Hating, detesting.

Abnegation (n.)—A denial; a renunciation; self-denial.

Ablution (n.)—In a general sense, the act of washing; a cleansing or purification by water. Appropriately, the washing of the body as a preparation for religious duties, enjoined by Moses and still practiced in many countries.

Abrogated (pp.)—Repealed; annulled by an act of authority.

Abstinence (n.)—In general, the act or practice of voluntarily refraining from or forbearing any action; more appropriately, the refraining from an indulgence of appetite or from customary gratifications of human propensities.

Acceded (pp.)—Agreed to or assented to something, such as a proposition or terms proposed by another person.

Acclamation (n.)—A shout of applause uttered by a multitude. Anciently, acclamation was a form of words that were uttered with vehemence, somewhat resembling a song, sometimes accompanied with applauses that were given by the hands.

Accretion (n.)—A growing together of separate things; an increase in size by natural growth; applied to the growth of an organic body by the increasing of its parts.

Addendum (n.)—Something added.

Adjure (v.)—To charge, bind, or command on oath or under the penalty of a curse; to charge earnestly and solemnly on pain of God's wrath.

Advent (n.)—The coming or arrival of the Lord. Christians celebrate the Advent holiday beginning four Sundays prior to Christmas Day.

Affectation (n.)—An attempt to assume or exhibit what is not natural or real; false pretense; artificial appearance.

Anathema (n.)—To place behind, backward, or at a distance; to separate. Excommunication with curses; hence, a curse or denunciation by ecclesiastical authority accompanying excommunication.

Annunciation (n.)—Literally, the noun that is derived from the verb *to announce.* It is also used specifically to refer to the angelic announcement of Jesus's birth.

Antediluvial (adj.)—Before the Flood in Noah's time; existing, happening, or relating to what happened before the Flood.

Aphorism (n.)—A maxim; a precept or principle expressed in few words; a detached sentence containing some important truth.

Apocrypha (n.)—The books that were excluded from the canonical scriptures (the Old and New Testaments) are referred to as the Apocrypha. Sometimes *Apocrypha* refers to books written during the New Testament period, and *Pseudepigrapha* refers to books written during the Old Testament period.

Appellation (n.)—Name; the word by which a thing is called and known.

Approbation (n.)—The act of approving; a liking; that state or disposition of the mind in which we assent to the propriety of a thing with some degree of pleasure or satisfaction; attestation; support.

Arrogate (v.)—To assume, demand, or challenge more than is proper; to make undue claims from vanity or false pretensions to right or merit.

Ascetic (n.)—Someone who intentionally lives a life of abstinence with regard to food or sexual intercourse. In the post–New Testament period, it came to refer to someone who was devoted exclusively to God and thus was pure or holy.

Asceticism (n.)—The life or habits of an ascetic involving unusual or extreme self-denial; ascetics are people who retire from the customary business of life and devote themselves to the duties of piety and devotion; hermits; recluses.

Ascribe (v.)—To attribute, impute, or assign; to consider or allege to belong, as in *to ascribe* perfection to God or imperfection to humans.

Asseveration (n.)—Positive affirmation or assertion; solemn declaration; not generally used for a declaration under oath but for a declaration accompanied with solemnity.

Assiduously (adv.)—Diligently; attentively; with earnestness and care.

Assuage (v.)—To abate, subside, or ease.

Attrition (n.)—Wearing or grinding down by friction; a gradual process of wearing down.

Audaciously (adv.)—In an impudent manner; with excess or boldness.

Avarice (n.)—An inordinate desire of gaining and possessing wealth; covetousness; greediness or insatiable desire of gain.

Averment (n.)—Affirmation; positive assertion; verification; establishment by evidence.

Basal (adj.)—Pertaining to the base; constituting the base.

Beneficence (n.)—The state or quality of being beneficent as exemplified in acts of kindness or charity.

Benign (adj.)—Kind; gracious; favorable; generous; wholesome; not pernicious, as a benign medicine; not malignant, as a benign disease.

Benighted (pp.)—Involved in darkness, whether physical or moral; overtaken by the night.

Betrothed (pp.)—Contracted, pledged, or promised to be the future spouse of another.

Bewailed (pp.), bewailing (ppr.)—(1) To mourn or bemoan the loss of someone or something. (2) Lamenting; bemoaning; expressing grief for.

Bereft (pp.)—Deprived; made destitute.

Bier (n.)—A carriage or frame of wood for conveying dead human bodies to the grave.

Bigotry (n.), bigoted (adj.), bigots (n.)—(1) Obstinate or blind attachment to a particular creed or to certain tenets; unreasonable zeal or warmth in favor of a party, sect, or opinion; excessive prejudice. (2) Obstinately and blindly attached to some creed, opinion, practice, or ritual; unreasonably devoted; illiberal toward the opinions of others. (3) People who are obstinately and unreasonably wedded to a particular religious creed, opinion, practice, or ritual.

Bower (n.)—A shelter or covered place in a garden, typically made with boughs of trees bent and twined together.

Bullock (n.)—An ox or castrated bull. In a scriptural sense, a bull is an enemy—powerful, fierce, and violent.

Cajole (v.)—To flatter; to soothe; to coax; to deceive or delude by flattery.

Caprice (n.)—A sudden change of opinion without reason; a whim or particular fancy.

Calumny (n.)—Slander; false accusation of a crime or offense, knowingly or maliciously made or reported, to the injury of another; false representation of facts reproachful to another, made by design and with knowledge of its falsehood.

Canon (n.), canonical (adj.)—(1) A law or rule in general; the authoritative books or epistles that are viewed as the holy scriptures according to a specific religious organization; a sanctioned or approved group or body of related literary works. (2) From the Greek word meaning a measuring stick, this term applies to the books of scripture that were determined to be authoritative and accepted as representative of the doctrines of the early Church.

Carnal (adj.)—Pertaining to flesh; fleshly; sensual; opposed to spiritual, such as carnal pleasure; being in the natural state; lecherous; lustful; given to sensual indulgence.

Casuistry (n.)—The science of resolving cases of doubtful propriety or of determining the lawfulness or unlawfulness of what a person may do by rules and principles drawn from the scriptures, from the laws of society, or from equity and natural reason.

Charger (n.)—The Greek word that is translated as *charger* in the New Testament refers to a platter, dish, or board.

Clarion (n.)—A kind of trumpet whose tube is narrower and whose tone is more acute and shrill than that of a common trumpet.

Conciliatory (adj.)—Tending to bring to a state of friendship; to reconcile; tending to make peace between persons at variance.

Condescend (v.)—To descend from the privileges of superior rank or dignity; to stoop or descend; to yield; to submit; implying a relinquishment of rank or dignity of character.

Congenital (adj.)—Present at birth; inborn; literally, of the same birth.

Consummate (v.), consummated (pp.), consummation (n.)—(1) To end; to finish by completing what was intended; to perfect; to bring or carry to the utmost point or degree. (2) Completed; perfected in some instances; ended. (3) Fulfillment; completion; end; perfection of a work, process, or scheme.

Contravention (n.)—Opposition; obstruction; contradiction; violation; infringement.

Contrite (adj.)—Literally, worn or bruised; hence, brokenhearted for sin; deeply affected with grief and sorrow for having offended God; humble; penitent.

Convivial (adj.)—Relating to a feast or entertainment; festal; social; jovial.

Corollary (n.)—Something that is proved by inference from something else already proved; inference; deduction; a natural consequence.

Corporeal (adj.)—Having a body; consisting of a material body; opposed to *spiritual* or *immaterial.*

Credulous (adj.)—Apt to believe without sufficient evidence; unsuspecting; easily deceived.

Culmination (n.)—The highest, climactic, or decisive point that marks the fulfillment, completion, or ending of an event.

Culpable (adj.)—Blamable; deserving censure, as the person who has done wrong or the act, conduct, or negligence of the person; sinful; criminal; immoral; faulty—but generally applied to acts less atrocious than crimes.

Debauched (pp.)—Corrupted; impaired in morals or purity of character.

Decalogue (n.)—The Ten Commandments or precepts given by God to Moses at Mount Sinai and originally written on two tables of stone.

Defile, defilement (v., n.), defileth (v.), defiling (ppr.)—(1) Like *desecrate,* these terms refer to the destruction of a sacred space or place; sin can defile the person, and unclean people can defile a sacred place. (2) To make unclean; to render foul or dirty; to make impure; to pollute; to make ceremonially unclean. (3) Polluting; making impure.

Deification (n.)—The act of deifying; the act of exalting to the rank of a god; the act of exalting into an object of worship or treating as an object of supreme regard.

Demoniac (n., adj.), demoniacal (adj.) —(1) A human being possessed by a demon; one whose volition and other mental faculties are overpowered, restrained, or disturbed in their regular operation by an evil spirit or a spiritual being of superior power. (2) Pertaining to demons or evil spirits.

Demur (v.)—To show approval or dislike; to take exception; to object; to suspend proceeding; to delay determination or conclusion.

Dereliction (n.)—The act of leaving with an intention not to reclaim; an utter forsaking; abandonment.

Desecration (n.)—The act of diverting from a sacred purpose or use to which a thing had been devoted; the act of abusing the sacredness of something.

Despotic (adj.)—Absolute in power; independent of control from humans, constitution, or laws; arbitrary in the exercise of power.

Diabolical (adj.)—Devilish; pertaining to the devil; hence, extremely malicious; nefarious; outrageously wicked; partaking of any quality ascribed to the devil.

Dirge (n.)—A song or tune intended to express grief, sorrow, or mourning.

Dolorous (adj.)—Painful, giving pain; expressing pain or grief, such as dolorous sighs.

Dropsical (adj.)—Diseased with dropsy or partaking of the nature of dropsy, which is an unnatural collection of water in any part of the body.

Dubiety (n.), dubious (adj.)—(1) Doubtfulness. (2) Doubtful; wavering or fluctuating in opinion; not settled; not determined; uncertain; not clear; of uncertain event or issue.

Ecclesiastical (adj.)—Pertaining or relating to matters of a Christian church, such as doctrine and practice, but more often referring to leadership and organization.

Efficacy (n.)—Power to produce effects; production of the effect intended; as the efficacy of the gospel in converting humans from sin or the efficacy of prayer.

Effulgent (adj.)—Shining; bright; splendid; diffusing a flood of life.

Egregiously (adv.)—Greatly; enormously; shamefully, usually in a bad sense.

Elucidated (pp.), elucidation (n.)—(1) Explained; made plain, clear, or intelligible. (2) The act of explaining or throwing light on any obscure subject; explanation; exposition; illustration.

Enmity (n.)—The quality of being an enemy; the opposite of friendship; ill will; hatred; unfriendly dispositions.

Enunciation (n.)—The act of uttering or pronouncing; expression; manner of utterance; declaration; open proclamation; public attestation.

Episcopate (n.)—A bishopric; the office and duty of a bishop.

Epithet (n.)—An adjective expressing some real quality of the thing to which it is applied; a descriptive expression; a word or phrase expressing some quality or attribute; a contemptuous word or phrase used in place of a person's name.

Epitome (n.)—An abridgment; a brief summary or abstract.

Eremitic (adj.)—Living in solitude or seclusion from the world; could be associated with the life of a hermit.

Erudite (adj.), erudition (n.)—(1) Having much knowledge; learned; scholarly. (2) Learning; much knowledge gained as a result of study or reading.

Espoused (pp.)—Betrothed; promised in marriage by contract.

Ethnarch (n.)—A local ruler appointed by Rome to rule in one of the provinces. The Herodians were ethnarchs, or rulers chosen from among the Jews.

Exigency (n.)—Demand; urgency; urgent need or want; pressing necessity; distress; any situation that demands immediate action or remedy.

Exorcism (n.)—The expulsion of evil spirits from a person via prayer or ceremony.

Expiate (v.), expiation (n.)—(1) To atone for; to make satisfaction for;

to extinguish the guilt of a crime by subsequent acts of piety or worship, by which the obligation to punish the crime is canceled. Among New Testament Jews, expiation was made chiefly by sacrifices or washings and purification. Among Christians, expiation for the sins of men and women is usually considered as having been made only by the obedience and sufferings of Christ. (2) The act of atoning for a crime; the act of making satisfaction for an offense by which the guilt is done away and the obligation of the offended person to punish the crime is canceled; atonement; satisfaction.

Festal (adj.)—Pertaining to a feast or festival; joyous; mirthful.

Fidelity (n.)—Faithfulness; careful and exact observance of duty or performance of obligations; firm adherence to a person or party with which someone is united; loyalty; observance of the marriage covenant; honesty; veracity; adherence to truth.

Fiend (n.), fiendish (adj.)—(1) An enemy in the worst sense; an implacable or malicious foe; the devil; an infernal being. (2) Extremely wicked, cruel, difficult, or troublesome; often associated with an enemy in the worst sense, an evil or wicked person, or an infernal being, especially Satan.

Filial (adj.)—Pertaining to a son or daughter; due from a son or daughter toward a mother or father; becoming a child in relation to parents.

Foreordained (adj.)—A calling that was extended prior to birth. Some events are also described in scripture as being planned and prepared.

Germane (adj.)—Pertinent; closely connected.

Gnosticism (n.)—The doctrines, principles, or system of philosophy taught by the Gnostics, a sect of philosophers who claimed to be the only ones who had a true knowledge of the Christian religion.

Gluttonous (adj.)—Given to excessive eating; indulging the appetite for food to excess.

Guile (n.), guileful (adj.), guileless (adj.)—(1) Craftiness or cunning. (2) Cunning; crafty; artful; wily; deceitful; insidious; treacherous; such as a guileful person. (3) Usually refers to a person whose actions are carried out without cunning but rather with frankness, sincerity, or honesty.

Harbinger (n.)—A forerunner or someone who goes ahead to prepare the way for others to follow; literally, it is the person who travels to the harbor to prepare for the arrival of a ship.

Heinous (adj.)—Extremely wicked, offensive, or hateful.

Hellenistic (adj.)—When Alexander the Great conquered the eastern Mediterranean, he did so under the guise of bringing Greek culture to the region. The influx of Greek culture is referred to as *Hellenism*. *Hellenistic* refers to all aspects of Greek culture, both as a time period and as a cultural influence.

Heresy (n.)—A fundamental error in religion or an error of opinion respecting some fundamental doctrine of religion. In countries that have an established religion, an opinion might be deemed heresy when it differs from that of the established religion. If the holy scriptures are the standard of faith, any opinion that is repugnant to their doctrines might be viewed as heresy.

Historicity (n.)—Real existence or occurrence; the quality of being real or documented as having actually happened.

Ignominious (adj.)—Literally meaning unnamed; by extension of that definition, it can also mean shameless and vile.

Ignominy (n.)—Public disgrace; shame; reproach; dishonor; infamy.

Imbibed (pp.)—Drunk in, such as a fluid; absorbed; received into the mind and retained.

Immaculate (adj.)—Sinless, pure, with a particular emphasis on being unstained from sin. Some Christians teach that Mary was immaculate or sinless when she gave birth to the Lord.

Impeccability (n.)—The quality of not being liable to sin; exemption from sin, error, or offense.

Impelled (pp.)—Driven forward; urged on; moved by any force or power, whether physical or moral.

Impenitent (adj., n.)—(1) Not repenting of sin; not contrite; of a hard heart. (2) One who does not repent; a hardened sinner.

Impertinent (adj.)—Not pertaining to the matter in hand; of no weight; having no bearing on the subject; rude; intrusive; meddling with that which does not belong to the person.

Impetuous (adj.), impetuosity (n.)—(1) Rushing with great force and violence; moving rapidly; furious; forcible; fierce; raging; vehement of mind. (2) A rushing with violence and great force; fury; violence.

Implacable (adj.)—Not to be appeased or subdued; incapable of being pacified and rendered peaceable; stubborn or constant in enmity.

Importunate (adj.), importuned (pp.), importunity (n.)—(1) Pressing or urging in request or demand; urgent in solicitation. (2) Requested with urgency; pressed with solicitation; urged with frequent or unceasing application. (3) Pressing solicitation; urgent request.

Impotent (adj.), impotently (adv.)—(1) Weak, feeble; wanting strength or power; unable by nature or disabled by disease, accident, or circumstances to perform any act. (2) Weakly; without power.

Imputation (n.)—The act of imputing, charging, or attributing, generally in an ill sense but sometimes in a good sense; charge or attribution of evil; censure; reproach.

Inalienable (adj.)—That which cannot be legally or justly alienated, given or taken away, or transferred to another.

Inanimate (adj.)—Destitute of animal life; lifeless.

Inaugurated (pp.), inauguration (n.)—(1) Installed in office with solemn ceremonies; initiated a formal beginning of. (2) The act of inducting into office with solemnity; investiture with office by appropriate ceremonies.

Incipiency (n.), incipient (adj.)—(1) Beginning; commencement. (2) Beginning; commencing.

Incongruous (adj.)—Unsuitable; not fitting; inconsistent; improper.

Incorporeal (adj.)—Not consisting of matter; not having a material body; immaterial. Humans tend to deem spirits as incorporeal substances.

Incredulous (adj.)—Not believing; indisposed to admit the truth of what is related; refusing or withholding belief.

Inculcated (pp.)—Impressed or enforced by frequent admonitions.

Incumbent (adj.)—Resting on a person as a duty or obligation; imposed and emphatically urging or pressing to performance; indispensable.

Ineffable (adj.)—Unspeakable; unutterable; that cannot be expressed in words.

Indigent (adj.)—Destitute of property or means of comfortable subsistence; needy; poor.

Indolence (n.)—Habitual idleness; indisposition to labor; inaction or want of exertion of body or mind proceeding from love of ease or aversion to toil.

Ineffaceable (adj.)—Incapable of being erased, rubbed out, or wiped out.

Ineptitude (n.)—Unfitness; unsuitableness.

Insidious (adj.)—Properly, lying in wait; hence, watching for an opportunity to ensnare or entrap; deceitful; sly; treacherous; working secretly or subtly.

Intercession (n.)—An entreaty or plea on behalf of another person; mediation in a dispute by an intermediary who reconciles differences.

Interment (n.)—The act of depositing a dead body in the earth; burial.

Intrinsic (adj.)—True; genuine; real; essential; inherent; not apparent or accidental.

Invective (n.)—A railing speech or expression; something uttered or written that is intended to cast censure or reproach on another; a harsh or reproachful accusation.

Investiture (n.)—Literally, the act of putting on clothes or getting dressed. The term refers to acting on someone else's behalf. In later times, it refers to the granting of offices by a civic leader.

Inveterate (adj.)—Deep rooted; firmly established by long continuance; obstinate.

Irreconcilable (adj.)—Two or more things that are not able to be reconciled, justified, or recalled to a state of friendship and kindness. In a scriptural sense, the effects of the Fall are irreconcilable with the requirement that we must be cleansed from sin to live with God. The Atonement reconciles the Fall.

Irredeemably (adv.)—Not capable of being redeemed or reformed; incapable of being rescued and delivered from the bondage of sin and the penalties of God's violated law.

Lasciviousness (n.)—Lustfulness; wantonness; indulgence of animal desires.

Latchet (n.)—A buckle or other means of fastening a shoe.

Levirate (n.)—The practice of marrying a widow to a brother of her deceased husband, as required by ancient Hebrew law.

Machinations (n.)—The act of planning or contriving schemes for executing some purposes, particularly evil purposes; artful designs formed with deliberation.

Magnificat (n.)—The song or hymn of Mary as recorded in Luke 1:46–55.

Malediction (n.)—Evil speaking; denunciation of evil; a cursing; slander.

Malfeasance (n.)—Evil doing; wrong; illegal deed.

Maligned (pp.)—Regarded with envy or malice; treated with extreme enmity; injured maliciously.

Mendacious (adj.)—Given to telling lies; lying; untruthful; false.

Mendicant (n.)—A beggar; one who begs alms.

Mishna (n.)—A written collection of the oral laws of the Pharisees that were written down beginning in the third century AD. The Mishna (now often spelled Mishnah) explains canonical scripture and preserves the traditions of the rabbis.

Munificence (n.)—A giving or bestowing liberally; bounty; liberality; to constitute *munificence,* the act of conferring must be free and proceed from generous motives.

Nefarious (adj.)—Wicked in the extreme; abominable; atrociously sinful or villainous; detestably vile.

Nomenclature (n.)—A list or catalog of the most usual and important words in a language with their meaning; a vocabulary or dictionary.

Nonplussed (pp.)—Puzzled; confounded; stopped by embarrassment.

Obduracy (n.), obdurate (adj.)—(1) Invincible hardness of heart; impenitence that cannot be subdued; inflexible persistency in sin; obstinacy in wickedness. (2) Hardened in heart; inflexibly hard; persisting obstinately in sin or impenitence; hardened against good or favor; stubborn; unyielding; inflexible.

Obsequious (adj.)—Promptly obedient or submissive to the will of another; compliant; servilely or meanly condescending; compliant to excess.

Olivet (adj.)—The adjective used to refer to the Mount of Olives or the discourse—Olivet discourse—thereon.

Omnipotent (adj.)—Almighty; possessing unlimited power; all powerful; one of the attributes of God.

Omniscience (n.), omniscient (adj.)—(1) An abstract noun meaning all knowledge; it typically refers to the quantity of knowledge but may also refer to the quality of knowledge. (2) Having universal knowledge or knowledge of all things; infinitely knowing; all seeing; one of the attributes of God.

Opprobrious (adj.), opprobrium (n.)—(1) Reproachful and contemptuous; scurrilous; blasted with infamy; despised; rendered hateful. (2) Reproach mingled with contempt or disdain.

Ostensibly (adv.)—Appearance in a manner that is declared or pretended.

Palliated (pp.)—Covered by excuses; eased; extenuated; softened by favorable representations.

Paroxysm (n.)—A fit of higher excitement or violence in a disease that has remissions or intermissions.

Paschal (adj.)—Referring to Passover (and later, Easter) with emphasis on the lamb, or Paschal Lamb, that was offered as part of the Jewish celebration of Passover.

Patrimony (n.)—A right or estate inherited from one's ancestors.

Penitent (adj.)—Suffering pain or sorrow of heart on account of sins, crimes, or offenses; contrite; sincerely affected by a sense of guilt and resolving to make amends.

Perdition (n.)—The utter loss of the soul or of final happiness in a future state; future misery or eternal death.

Perennial (adj.)—Lasting or continuing without cessation through the year; perpetual; unceasing; never failing; continuing without intermission, as a fever.

Perfidious (adj.), perfidy (n.)—(1) Violating good faith or vows; false to trust or confidence reposed; treacherous; proceeding from treachery or consisting in breach of faith; guilty of violated allegiance. (2) The act of violating faith, a promise, vow, or allegiance; treachery; the violation of a trust reposed.

Pernicious (adj.)—Destructive; having the quality of killing, destroying, or injuring; very injurious or mischievous.

Pertinence, pertinency (n.), pertinent (adj.)—(1) Justness of relation to the subject or matter in hand; fitness; suitableness. (2) Related to the subject or matter in hand; just to the purpose; adapted to the end proposed; not foreign to the thing intended.

Phylactery (n.)—Among the Jews, a slip of parchment on which was written some text of scripture, particularly of the Decalogue (the Ten Commandments given by God to Moses at Mount Sinai), worn by devout persons on the forehead, breast, or neck as a mark of their religion.

Pious (adj.)—Godly; reverencing and honoring God in heart and in the practice of the duties He has enjoined; having due veneration and affection for the character of God and habitually obeying His commands; religious; devoted to the service of God.

Plenitude (n.)—Fulness; completeness.

Portent (n.), portentous (adj.)—(1) A warning of coming evil; a previous sign or omen indicating the approach of evil or calamity. (2) Indicating evil to come; ominous; wonderful, amazing, or extraordinary in an evil sense.

Precocious (adj.)—Developed earlier than usual in knowledge, skill, and so forth before the proper or natural time; premature.

Prerogative (n.)—An exclusive or peculiar privilege; a right or privilege that nobody else has; special superiority of right or privilege that is derived from an official position of power.

Presage (v.)—To forebode; to foreshow; to indicate by some present fact what is to follow or come to pass; to foretell; to predict; to prophesy.

Privation (n.)—The state of being deprived; particularly, deprivation or absence of what is necessary for comfort; the act of removing something possessed.

Promulgator (n.)—A publisher; a person who makes known or teaches publicly what was before unknown.

Propitiation (n.), propitious (adj.)—(1) An offering, usually with an emphasis on appeasing God or offering a reconciliation for sin. (2) Favorable; kind (applied to men); disposed to be gracious or merciful; ready to forgive sins and bestow blessings (applied to God).

Proscription (n.)—A condemnation of someone or something that is usually based on a legal decision. A proscription can generally refer to a sentence of death.

Provocation (n.)—Anything that excites anger; the cause of resentment; the act of exciting anger.

Puerile (adj.)—Childish; youthful; juvenile; trifling; foolish for an adult to say or do.

Querulously (adv.)—In a complaining or murmuring manner.

Rabbinical (adj.)—Pertaining to Jewish rabbis or to their opinions, learning, writings, or language. A rabbi is an ordained teacher of Jewish law and religion who usually serves as the spiritual leader of a Jewish congregation.

Reconciliation (n.)—The act of reconciling parties at variance (or restoring to friendship or favor); renewal of friendship after disagreement or enmity; the means by which sinners are reconciled and brought into a state of favor with God after natural estrangement or enmity; the Atonement; expiation.

Refutation (n.)—The act or process of refuting or disproving; the act of proving to be false or erroneous; the overthrowing of an argument, opinion, testimony, doctrine, or theory by argument or countervailing proof.

Rejoinder (n.)—An answer to a reply or, in general, an answer; in law pleadings, the defendant's answer to the plaintiff's query.

Replete (adj.)—Completely filled; full; abundantly supplied.

Resplendent (adj.)—Very bright; shining with brilliant luster.

Reprobate (n., adj.)—Abandoned in sin, error, or apostasy; lost to virtue or grace.

Repudiated (pp.)—Rejected; discarded; cast off or disowned; divorced.

Requisite (adj.)—Required by the nature of things or by circumstances; necessary; so needful that it cannot be dispensed with.

Retribution (n.)—Repayment; return according to the action; reward; compensation; the distribution of rewards and punishments at the Day of Judgment.

Ribald (adj.), ribaldry (n.)—(1) Low; base; mean. (2) Mean, vulgar language; chiefly, obscene language.

Sacerdotal (adj.)—Pertaining to priests or the priesthood; priestly. The noun *sacerdotalism* refers to the belief that priests act as mediators between God and humans.

Sanctimonious (adj.)—Putting on the airs of sanctity; having the appearance of holiness, goodness, purity, godliness, sacredness, or solemnity.

Sceptre (n.)—British spelling of *scepter;* a staff borne by kings on solemn occasions as a badge of authority; the appropriate ensign of royalty; associated with royal power or authority.

Scrupulosity (n.), scrupulous (adj.), scrupulously (adv.)—(1) The caution or tenderness arising from the fear of doing wrong or offending. (2) Nicely doubtful; hesitating to determine or to act; cautious in decision from a fear of offending or doing wrong. (3) With a nice regard to minute particulars or to exact propriety.

Secular (adj.)—Everything that is not sacred or spiritual. It can refer generally to the world.

Sedition (n.)—A factious commotion of the people or a tumultuous assembly of the people rising in opposition to law or the administration of justice and in disturbance of the public peace; in general, sedition is a local or limited insurrection in opposition to civil authority.

Septuagint (n.)—Literally, "the seventy." The term refers to the translation of the Old Testament into Greek. According to legend, seventy translators worked on the project. Today, it is often viewed as being inferior to the Hebrew Old Testament.

Similitude (n.)—A likeness or comparison of two things that are similar.

Solicitous (adj.)—Showing care or concern; anxious; desirous or eager to please.

Sophistries (n.)—Fallacious reasoning; reasoning sound in appearance only.

Spikenard (n.)—An aromatic plant; the oil or ointment procured from the species of plant commonly referred to as nard or muskroot.

Spoliation (n.)—The act of plundering or committing robbery.

Stultify (v.)—To make foolish or absurd; to reduce to absurdity; to make someone a fool.

Subserviency (n.)—Great politeness and obedience, such as exhibited by a slave; tame submissiveness; the act of being of use or service; subservience.

Sumptuous (adj.), sumptuously (adv.)—(1) Costly; expensive; splendid; magnificent. (2) Expensively, splendidly; with great magnificence.

Supererogation (n.)—Performance of more than is required by duty, obligation, or need.

Superfluous (adj.)—More than is wanted or sufficient; rendered unnecessary by superabundance.

Superlative (adj.)—Highest in degree; most eminent; surpassing all other; supreme.

Superscription (n.)—That which is written or engraved on the outside or above something else; an impression of letters on coins.

Superseding (ppr.)—Making void or useless by superior power or by coming in the place of; setting aside; rendering unnecessary; suspending.

Supplication (n.)—Entreaty; humble and earnest prayer in worship; petition; earnest request.

Synoptic (adj.)—Giving a general view of the whole or of the principal parts of a thing; taking a common view as in Matthew, Mark, and Luke because they are much alike in content, order, and approach.

Temerity (n.)—Rashness; unreasonable contempt of danger; extreme boldness.

Tenaciously (adv.)—With a disposition to hold fast what is possessed; adhesively; obstinately; with firm adherence.

Tenuous (adj.)—Small; minute; thin; having little substance.

Tetrarch (n.)—A Roman governor of the fourth part of a province; a subordinate prince.

Theocracy (n.)—Government of a state by the immediate direction of God or the state thus governed; the Israelites of the Old Testament are a good example.

Theophany (n.)—A visible manifestation or appearance of a deity, in this case referring to Jesus Christ.

Tractate (n.)—A treatise; a tract or a small book or pamphlet on a religious or political subject; now an obsolete term.

Transcendent (adj.)—Excellent; superior or supreme in excellence; surpassing ordinary limits; extraordinary.

Transient (adj.)—Of short duration; not permanent; not lasting or durable.

Transitory (adj.)—Passing without continuance; continuing a short time; fleeting; speedily vanishing.

Transmutation (n.)—The changing of something from one state to another, such as Jesus's changing water into wine.

Trenchant (adj.)—Cutting; sharp; vigorous; effective; clear-cut; distinct.

Trepidation (n.)—An involuntary trembling; a quaking or quivering, particularly from fear or terror; a state of terror.

Targum (n.)—The translation of the Hebrew scriptures (the Old

Testament) into Aramaic, the popular language of the Jews at the time of Jesus.

Tribunal (n.)—A court or minister of justice.

Umbrage (n.), umbrageous (adj.)—(1) Suspicion of injury; offense; resentment. (2) Shady; shaded; the foliage of trees providing shade.

Unfilial (adj.)—Unsuitable to a son or child; undutiful; not becoming a child.

Unsated (adj.)—Not satisfied.

Vacillate (v.)—To waver; to move one way and the other; to fluctuate in mind or opinion; to be unsteady or inconstant.

Vagary (n.)—A wondering of the thoughts; a whim; a whimsical purpose.

Veneration (n.)—The highest degree of respect and reverence; respect mingled with some degree of awe; a feeling or sentiment excited by the dignity and superiority of a person or by the sacredness of that person's character.

Vestige (n.)—The mark or remains of something; a slight remnant; a trace.

Vicarious (adj.), vicariously (adv.)—Acting for another; filling the place of another; by substitution.

Vicissitude (n.)—Regular change or succession of one thing to another; change in fortune or circumstances; revolution.

Vindicate (v.), vindication (n.), vindictive (adj.)—(1) To justify; to support or maintain as true or correct against denial, censure, or objections; to defend with success; to prove to be just or valid. (2) The act of supporting by proof or legal process; the proving of something to be just. (3) Revengeful; given to revenge.

Virile (adj.)—Belonging to or characteristic of a man; manly; masculine; full of manly strength or masculine vigor.

Vitiate (v.)—To injure the substance or qualities of a thing so as to impair or spoil its use and value; to render defective; to destroy.

Viviate (v.)—To make alive or to infuse someone with life.

Vociferous (adj.)—Making a loud outcry; clamorous; noisy.

SELECTED SOURCES

STUDY GUIDES

Bennion, Lowell L. "A Series of Twelve Articles to Support the Gospel Doctrine Course 'Jesus the Christ.'" *Instructor,* November 1963, 406–10; December 1963, 436–39; January 1964, 38–42; February 1964, 80–83; March 1964, 120–24; April 1964, 164–67; May 1964, 196–99, 201; June 1964, 242–45, 247; July 1964, 285–87; August 1964, 322–25; September 1964, 368–71; and October 1964, 408–11. Cited as 1963–64 Study Guide.

Riddle, Chauncey C. *Guide for Instructors for the Melchizedek Priesthood Course of Study 1963, Jesus the Christ.* Salt Lake City: The Church of Jesus Christ of Latter-day Saints, 1963.

Study for the Melchizedek Priesthood and Priests. Salt Lake City: The Church of Jesus Christ of Latter-day Saints, 1916.

OTHER PUBLISHED WORKS

Davidson, Karen Lynn, David J. Whittaker, Richard L. Jensen, and Mark Ashurst-McGee, eds. *Histories, Volume 1: Joseph Smith*

Histories, 1832–1844. Vol. 1 of the Histories series of *The Joseph Smith Papers,* edited by Dean C. Jessee, Ronald K. Esplin, and Richard Lyman Bushman. Salt Lake City: Church Historian's Press, 2012.

Ehat, Andrew F., and Lindon W. Cook, comps. and eds. *The Words of Joseph Smith: The Contemporary Accounts of the Nauvoo Discourses of the Prophet Joseph Smith.* Provo, Utah: BYU Religious Studies Center, 1980.

Jackson, Kent P. *The Book of Moses and the Joseph Smith Translation Manuscripts.* Provo, Utah: BYU Religious Studies Center, 2005.

————, ed. *Joseph Smith's Commentary on the Bible.* Salt Lake City: Deseret Book, 1994.

Jessee, Dean C., Mark Ashurst-McGee, and Richard L. Jensen, eds. *Journals, Volume 1:1832–1839.* Vol. 1 of the Journals series of *The Joseph Smith Papers,* edited by Dean C. Jessee, Ronald K. Esplin, and Richard Lyman Bushman. Salt Lake City: Church Historian's Press, 2008.

Romney, Marion G. "The Book 'Jesus the Christ.'" *Improvement Era,* November 1962, 804–5, 866–68.

Talmage, James E. *Jesus the Christ: A Study of the Messiah and His Mission according to Holy Scriptures Both Ancient and Modern.* Salt Lake City: The Church of Jesus Christ of Latter-day Saints, 1973, 1981.

Talmage, John R. "An Assignment: Its Fulfillment." *Improvement Era,* November 1962, 806–9.

————. *The Talmage Story: Life of James E. Talmage—Educator, Scientist, Apostle.* Salt Lake City: Bookcraft, 1972.

Wayment, Thomas A. *The Complete Joseph Smith Translation of the New Testament.* Salt Lake City: Deseret Book, 2005.

Zobell, Albert L., Jr. "The Life of James E. Talmage." *Improvement Era,* November 1962, 812–14.